PINEAPPLE CROCHET DESIGNS

edited by
RITA WEISS

Dover Publications, Inc.
New York

Copyright © 1980 by Dover Publications, Inc.
All rights reserved under Pan American and International Copyright Conventions.

Published in Canada by General Publishing Company, Ltd., 30 Lesmill Road, Don Mills, Toronto, Ontario.
Published in the United Kingdom by Constable and Company, Ltd., 10 Orange Street, London WC2H 7EG.

This Dover edition, first published in 1980, is a new selection of patterns from *Ruffled Doilies and the Pansy Doily. Star Book 59*, published by the American Thread Company in 1948; *The Pick of the Pineapples, Book No. 237*, published in 1952 by the Spool Cotton Company; *Chair Sets, Book No. 206*, published in 1944 by the Spool Cotton Company; *Edgings, Book No. 236*, published in 1947 by the Spool Cotton Company; *Crochet for Small Fry. Sizes 2, 3, 4 Dresses*, published in 1944 by the Spool Cotton Company; *Doilies, Book No. 235*, published in 1947 by the Spool Cotton Company; *Hand Crochet by Royal Society. Crisp New Doilies, Book No. 9*, published in 1948 by the Royal Society, Inc.; *Crocheted Bedspreads*, published in 1948 by the Lily Mills Company; *Pineapple Fan-Fair, Book No. 266*, published in 1950 by the Spool Cotton Company; *Featuring 14 New Pineapple Designs, Book No. 230*, published in 1946 by the Spool Cotton Company. A new introduction has been written especially for this edition.

International Standard Book Number: 0-486-23939-X
Library of Congress Catalog Card Number: 79-57222

Manufactured in the United States of America
Dover Publications, Inc.
31 East 2nd Street
Mineola, N.Y. 11501

Introduction

There is certainly no need to take a poll to determine America's most popular crochet design. It is the pineapple!

Like all crocheted lace, the pineapple design is a real investment in beauty because it wears practically forever, and remains a classic long after other fashions have come and gone. The pineapple design blends with furniture from any period; it is as fitting for a colonial setting as for a modern home. It combines equally as well with formal or informal settings.

This is a new collection of some of the most lovely pineapple patterns published in instruction brochures over thirty years ago, during a period when the making of hand-crocheted lace was an extremely popular pastime. There are patterns here for the master crocheter who is ready to undertake a large project such as a pineapple tablecloth, for the inveterate crocheter who will find such unusual pineapple projects as a set of pineapple lampshades, for the novice in the art of the crochet hook who can learn her first lessons while making a beautiful and useful pineapple doily, and for those who feel a crocheted item is a creative expression that transcends mere functionalism.

Since the patterns in this book all come from old instruction brochures, many of the threads listed with the patterns may no longer be available. Other threads of similar weight which will produce the same gauge may be substituted. Check with your local needlework shop or department. Whatever type of thread you decide to use, be certain to buy at one time sufficient thread of the same dye lot to complete the project you wish to make. It is often impossible to match shades later as dye lots vary.

For best results the number of stitches and rows should correspond with those indicated in the directions. Before starting any project, make a sample of the stitch, working with the suggested hook and the desired thread. If your working tension is too tight or too loose, use a coarser or finer crochet hook to obtain the correct gauge.

When you have completed your project, it should be washed and blocked. No matter how carefully you have worked, blocking will give your pineapple project a "professional" look. Use a good netural soap or detergent and make suds in warm water. Wash by squeezing the suds through the project, but do not rub. Rinse two or three times in clear water, if desired. Starching the project will give it a crisper look. Following the measurements given with the pattern, and using rustproof pins, pin the article right side down on a well-padded surface. Be sure to pin out all picots, loops, scallops, etc., along the outside edges. When the project is almost completely dry, press through a damp cloth with a moderately hot iron. Do not rest the iron on the decorative, raised stitches! When thoroughly dry, remove the pins.

The crochet terminology and hooks listed in this book are those used in the United States. The following charts give the U.S. name of crochet stitches and their equivalents in other countries and the equivalents to U.S. crochet hook sizes. Crocheters should become thoroughly familiar with the differences in both crochet terms and hook sizes before starting any project.

STITCH CONVERSION CHART

U.S. Name	Equivalent
Chain	Chain
Slip	Single crochet
Single crochet	Double crochet
Half-double or short-double crochet	Half-treble crochet
Double crochet	Treble crochet
Treble crochet	Double-treble crochet
Double-treble crochet	Treble-treble crochet
Treble-treble or long-treble crochet	Quadruple-treble crochet
Afghan stitch	Tricot crochet

HOOK CONVERSION CHART

Aluminum

U.S. Size	B	C	D	E	F	G	H	I	J	K
British & Canadian Size	12	11	10	9	8	7	5	4	3	2
Metric Size	2½	3	—	3½	4	4½	5	5½	6	7

Steel

U.S. Size	00	0	1	2	3	4	5	6
British & Canadian Size	000	00	0	1	—	1½	2	2½

All of the stitches and the abbreviations used in the projects in this book are explained on page 45.

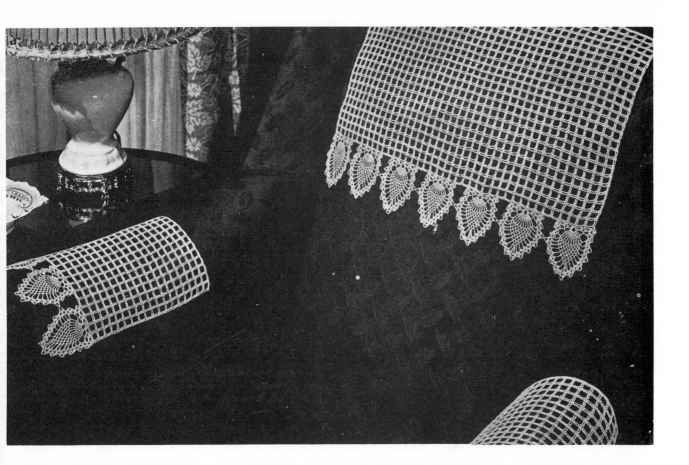

Pineapple Luncheon Set & Chair Back

RECTANGULAR LUNCHEON SET

MATERIALS: J. & P. Coats or Clark's O.N.T. Best Six Cord Mercerized Crochet, Size 20: **Small Ball**: J. & P. Coats—6 balls of *White or Ecru, or* Clark's O.N.T.—9 balls of *White or Ecru . . . Steel Crochet Hook No. 9.*

GAUGE: 4 sps make 1¾ inches.

Place Doily measures 11 x 17 inches

PLACE DOILY (Make 2) . . .
Starting at one short end, make a chain about 15 inches long (12 ch sts to 1 inch). **1st row:** Sc in 2nd ch from hook, sc in next ch, * ch 4, skip 4 ch, sc in next 2 ch. Repeat from * across until there are 28 sps, ending with 2 sc. Cut off remaining chain. Ch 4, turn. **2nd row:** Skip 1st sc, tr in next sc, * ch 4, tr in next 2 sc. Repeat from * across. Ch 1, turn. **3rd row:** Sc in first 2 tr, * ch 4, sc in next 2 tr. Repeat from * across. Ch 4, turn.

Repeat the 2nd and 3rd rows alternately until piece measures 12 inches, ending with the 3rd row. Ch 5, turn.

FIRST PINEAPPLE . . . 1st row:
Skip 1st sc, in next sc make 2 dc, ch 2 and 2 dc (shell made); skip 4 ch and 1 sc, shell in next sc, skip 4 ch and 1 sc, in next sc make 2 dc, ch 5 and 2 dc; (skip 4 ch and 1 sc, shell in

next sc) twice. Ch 5, turn. **2nd row:** In sp of next shell make a shell (shell made over shell), ch 2, sc in sp of next shell, ch 2, 10 tr in ch-5 sp of next shell, ch 2, sc in sp of next shell, ch 2, shell over next shell. Ch 5, turn. **3rd row:** Shell over shell, ch 2, (tr in next tr, ch 1) 9 times; tr in next tr, ch 2, shell over shell. Ch 5, turn. **4th row:** Shell over shell, ch 4, sc in next ch-1 sp, (ch 3, sc in next sp) 8 times; ch 4, shell over shell. Ch 5, turn. **5th row:** Shell over shell, ch 4, sc in next ch-3 loop, (ch 3, sc in next loop) 7 times; ch 4, shell over shell. Ch 5, turn. Work in this manner, having 1 less ch-3 loop on each row until 1 loop remains. Ch 5, turn. **Next row:** Shell over shell, ch 4, sc in ch-3 loop, ch 4, 2 dc in sp of next shell, ch 1, sl st in sp of last shell, ch 1, 2 dc in same place as last 2 dc, ch 5, turn, sl st in joining of shells. Break off.

SECOND PINEAPPLE . . . Skip 4 ch, 2 sc, 4 ch and 1 sc; attach thread to next sc, ch 5, shell in same sc, skip 4 ch and 1 sc, shell in next sc, skip 4 ch and 1 sc, in next sc make 2 dc, ch 5 and 2 dc; (skip 4 ch and 1 sc, shell in next sc) twice. Ch 5, turn. Complete pineapple as before. Work 3 more pineapples across this edge. Sew the 3rd loop of each adjacent pineapple neatly together. Work across opposite side to correspond.

CENTER DOILY . . . Work exactly as for Place Doily.

CHAIR SET

MATERIALS: J. & P. Coats or Clark's O.N.T. Best Six Cord Mercerized Crochet, *Size 20:* **Small Ball**: J. & P. Coats—5 balls of *White or Ecru, or* Clark's O.N.T.—7 balls of *White or Ecru . . . Steel Crochet Hook No. 9.*

GAUGE: 4 sps make 1¾ inches.

Chair Back measures 13 x 17½ inches; each Arm Piece 7 x 11 inches

CHAIR BACK . . . Starting at top make a chain about 20 inches long (12 ch sts to 1 inch). **1st row:** Sc in 2nd ch from hook, sc in next ch, * ch 4, skip 4 ch, sc in next 2 ch. Repeat from * across until there are 40 sps, ending with 2 sc. Cut off remaining chain. Ch 4, turn. Work as for Luncheon Set until piece measures 10½ inches, ending with the 3rd row. Ch 5, turn. Work 7 pineapples across lower edge only as for Luncheon Set.

ARM PIECE (Make 2) . . . Starting at one short end, make a chain about 10 inches long (12 ch sts to 1 inch) and work as for Chair Back until there are 16 sps. Cut off remaining chain. Ch 4, turn. Work as for Luncheon Set until piece measures 8 inches, ending with the 3rd row. Work 3 pineapples across lower edge only as for Luncheon Set.

Pineapple Ruffle

Materials Required: AMERICAN THREAD COMPANY "STAR" MERCERIZED CROCHET COTTON, ARTICLE 20 Size 20

3—250 yd. Balls White, Ecru or Cream.
Steel Crochet Hook No. 12.
Doily measures about 13 inches in diameter without the ruffle.
Ch 6, join to form a ring, ch 1 and work 8 s c in ring, join in 1st s c.

2nd Row. * Ch 10, s c in next s c, repeat from * 6 times, ch 4, d tr c (3 times over needle) in next s c. This brings thread in position for next row.

3rd Row. Ch 3, 2 d c in same space, * ch 7, 3 d c in next loop, repeat from * all around, ch 7, join.

4th Row. Sl st to next d c, * ch 5, 3 d c in next loop, ch 5, s c in center d c of next d c group, repeat from * all around ending row with ch 5, 3 d c in next loop, ch 2, tr c in same space with sl st.

5th Row. * Ch 7, s c in next loop, repeat from * all around ending row with ch 3, tr c in tr c.

6th Row. Ch 5, d c in same space, * ch 5, 1 d c, ch 3, 1 d c in center st of next loop, repeat from * all around, ch 5, join in 3rd st of ch.

7th Row. Sl st into loop, ch 3, d c in same space, ch 3, 2 d c in same space, * ch 3, skip 1 loop, 8 tr c in next loop, ch 3, skip 1 loop, 2 d c, ch 3, 2 d c (shell) in next loop, repeat from * all around ending row with ch 3, skip 1 loop, 8 tr c in next loop, ch 3, join in 3rd st of ch.

8th Row. Sl st into center of shell, ch 3, d c in same space, ch 3, 2 d c in same space, * ch 3, 1 tr c in each tr c with ch 1 between each tr c, ch 3, 2 d c, ch 3, 2 d c (shell) in center of next shell, repeat from * all around ending row with ch 3, 1 tr c in each tr c with ch 1 between each tr c, ch 3, join in 3rd st of ch.

9th Row. Sl st to center of shell, ch 3, 1 d c, ch 3, 2 d c in same space, ** ch 4, s c between 1st 2 tr c of pineapple, * ch 4, s c between next 2 tr c, repeat from * 5 times, ch 4, 2 d c, ch 3, 2 d c in center of next shell, repeat from ** all around in same manner, join.

10th Row. Sl st to center of shell, ch 3, 1 d c, ch 3, 2 d c in same space,'** ch 4, skip 1 loop, s c in 1st loop of pineapple, * ch 4, s c in next loop, repeat from * 4 times, ch 4, shell in shell, repeat from ** all around in same manner, join.

11th Row. Sl st to center of shell, ch 3, 1 d c, ch 3, 2 d c, ch 3, 2 d c in same space, **ch 4, s c in 1st loop of pineapple, * ch 4, s c in next loop, repeat from * 3 times, ch 4, 2 d c, ch 3, 2 d c, ch 3, 2 d c in center of next shell, repeat from ** all around in same manner, join.

12th Row. Sl st into loop, ch 3, 1 d c, ch 3, 2 d c in same space, ** ch 5, shell in next loop, ch 4, s c in 1st loop of pineapple, * ch 4, s c in next loop, repeat from * twice, ch 4, skip 1 loop, shell in next ch 3 loop, repeat from ** all around in same manner, join.

13th Row. Sl st to center of shell, shell in same space, ** ch 3, shell in next loop, ch 3, shell in next shell, ch 4, s c in 1st loop of pineapple, * ch 4, s c in next loop, repeat from * once, ch 4, shell in next shell, repeat from ** all around in same manner, join.

14th Row. Sl st to center of shell, shell in same space, * ch 3, 1 d c, ch 3, 1 d c in next loop, ch 3, shell in next shell, ch 3, 1 d c, ch 3, 1 d c in next loop, ch 3, shell in next shell, ch 4, s c in 1st loop of pineapple, ch 4, s c in next loop, ch 4, shell in next shell, repeat from * all around in same manner, join.

15th Row. Sl st to center of shell, shell in same space, * ch 4, skip 1 loop, 8 tr c in next loop, ch 4, shell in next shell, ch 4, skip 1 loop, 8 tr c in next loop, ch 4, shell in next shell, ch 4, s c in remaining loop of pineapple, ch 4, shell in next shell, repeat from * all around in same manner, join.

16th Row. Sl st to center of shell, shell in same space, * ch 4, 1 tr c in each of the next 8 tr c with ch 1 between each tr c, ch 4, shell in next shell, ch 4, 1 tr c in each of the next 8 tr c with ch 1 between each tr c, ch 4, shell in next shell, shell in next shell, repeat from * all around in same manner ending row to correspond, join in 3rd st of ch of 1st shell, ch 1, turn.

17th Row. Sl st back to center of shell just made, ch 3, turn, d c in same space, ch 2, 2 d c in center of next shell, ** ch 4, s c between 1st 2 tr c, * ch 4, s c between next 2 tr c, repeat from * 5 times, ch 4, shell in next shell, ch 4, s c between 1st 2 tr c, * ch 4, s c between next 2 tr c, repeat from * 5 times, ch 4, 2 d c in center of next shell, ch 2, 2 d c in center of next shell, repeat from **all around in same manner, join.

18th Row. Sl st into ch 2 loop, shell in same space, ** ch 4, s c in 1st loop of pineapple, * ch 4, s c in next loop, repeat from * 4 times, ch 4, shell in next shell, ch 4, s c in 1st loop of next pineapple, * ch 4, s c in next loop, repeat from * 4 times, ch 4, shell in next ch 2 loop, repeat from ** all around in same manner, join.

19th Row. Sl st to center of shell, ch 3, 1 d c, ch 3, 2 d c, ch 3, 2 d c in same space, ** ch 4, s c in 1st loop of pineapple, * ch 4, s c in next loop, repeat from * 3 times, ch 4, 2 d c, ch 3, 2 d c, ch 3, 2 d c in center of next shell, repeat from ** all around in same manner, join.

20th Row. Sl st to loop, shell in same space, ** ch 5, shell in next ch 3 loop, ch 4, s c in 1st loop of pineapple, * ch 4, s c in next loop, repeat from * twice, ch 4, shell in next ch 3 loop, repeat from ** all around in same manner, join.

21st Row. Sl st to center of shell, shell in same space, ** ch 4, s c in next loop, ch 4, shell in center of next shell, ch 4, s c in 1st loop of pineapple, * ch 4, s c in next loop, repeat from *, ch 4, shell in next shell, repeat from ** all around in same manner, join.

22nd Row. Sl st to center of shell, shell in same space, * ch 5, s c in next s c, ch 5, shell in next shell, ch 4, s c in 1st loop of pineapple, ch 4, s c in next loop, ch 4, shell in next shell, repeat from * all around in same manner, join.

23rd Row. Sl st to center of shell, shell in same space, ** ch 7, * thread over needle twice, insert in next loop, thread over and work off 2 loops twice, repeat from *, thread over and work off all loops at one time, ch 7, shell

in next shell, ch 4, s c in remaining loop of pineapple, ch 4, shell in next shell, repeat from ** all around in same manner, join.

24th Row. Sl st to center of shell, shell in same space, * ch 7, s c in next loop, ch 9, s c in next loop, ch 7, shell in next shell, ch 4, s c in next s c at top of pineapple, ch 4, shell in next shell, repeat from * all around in same manner, join.

25th Row. Sl st to center of shell, shell in same space, * ch 7, s c in next loop, ch 7, s c in next loop, ch 7, s c in next loop, ch 7, shell in next shell, ch 1, shell in next shell, repeat from * all around in same manner, join.

26th Row. Sl st to center of shell, ch 3, d c in same space, ** ch 7, s c in next loop, * ch 7, s c in next loop, repeat from * twice, ch 7, 2 d c in center of next shell, 2 d c in center of next shell, repeat from ** all around ending row with 2 d c in last shell, join.

27th Row. ** Ch 7, s c in next loop, * ch 7, s c in next loop, repeat from * 3 times, ch 7, s c in center of 4 d c group, repeat from ** all around ending row with ch 3, tr c in center of 4 d c group.

28th Row. * Ch 8, s c in next loop, repeat from * all around ending row with ch 3, tr c in tr c.

29th Row. Ch 3, 2 d c in same space, * ch 5, 3 d c in next loop, repeat from * all around, join.

30th Row. Sl st to center of loop, * ch 8, s c in next loop, repeat from * all around ending row with ch 3, tr c in sl st.

31st Row. Ch 3, 2 d c in same space, * ch 6, 3 d c in next loop, repeat from * all around ending row with ch 3, tr c in 3rd st of ch.

32nd Row. * Ch 9, s c in next loop, repeat from * all around ending row with ch 3, d tr c in tr c.

33rd Row. Same as 31st row but ending row with ch 1, tr tr c (4 times over needle) in 3rd st of ch.

RUFFLE. * Ch 10, s c in same loop, ch 10, s c in same loop, ch 10, s c in same loop, ch 10, s c in next loop, repeat from * all around ending row with ch 5, tr tr c in same space as beginning (384 loops).

2nd Row. * Ch 10, s c in next loop, repeat from * all around ending row same as last row. Repeat the 2nd row twice but ending the last row with ch 3, thread over needle 5 times, thread over and work off all loops 2 at a time.

5th Row. Ch 4, 7 tr c in same loop, * ch 6, 4 s c in next loop, 4 s c in next loop, ch 6, 8 tr c in next loop, repeat from * all around ending row with ch 6, 4 s c in each of the next 2 loops, ch 6, join in 4th st of ch.

6th Row. Ch 5, 1 tr c in each of the next 7 tr c with ch 1 between each tr c, * ch 8, skip 2 s c, 1 s c in each of the next 4 s c, ch 8, 1 tr c in each of the next 8 tr c with ch 1 between each tr c, repeat from * all around ending row with ch 8, skip 2 s c, 1 s c in each of the next 4 s c, ch 8, join in 4th st of ch.

7th Row. Sl st between 1st 2 tr c, ** ch 7, sl st in 4th st from hook for picot, ch 3, s c between next 2 tr c, * ch 7, sl st in 4th st from hook for picot, ch 3, s c between next 2 tr c, repeat from * 4 times, ch 6, s c in next loop, ch 9, sl st in 5th st from hook for picot, ch 4, sl st in same space for picot, ch 4, sl st in same space for picot (a 3 picot cluster) ch 4, s c in next loop, ch 6, s c between first 2 tr c of next tr c group, repeat from ** all around, break thread.

Directions for Starching

STARCH: Dissolve ¼ cup starch in ½ cup of cold water. Boil slowly over a low flame, as it thickens stir in gradually about 1¼ cups of cold water. Boil, stirring constantly until starch clears. This makes a thick pasty mixture.
As soon as starch is cool enough to handle, dip doily and squeeze starch through it thoroughly. Wring out extra starch. The doily should be wet with starch but there should be none in the spaces. Pin center of doily in position according to size and leave until thoroughly dry. If steam iron is used iron ruffle after it is dry. If regular iron is used dampen ruffle slightly before pressing. Pin folds of ruffle in position and leave until thoroughly dry.

Pineapple Doily

ROYAL SOCIETY SIX CORD CORDICHET,

Size 30, 2 balls of White or Ecru. Steel Crochet Hook No. 10.

Doily measures 11½ inches in diameter.

Starting at center, ch 12. Join with sl st to form ring. **1st rnd:** Ch 3, 23 dc in ring. Join with sl st to 3rd st of ch-3. **2nd rnd:** Sc in same place as sl st, (ch 6, skip 3 dc, sc in next dc) 6 times; sl st in first sc. **3rd rnd:** In each sp around make sc, half dc, dc, 4 tr, dc, half dc and sc. Join to first sc (6 petals). **4th rnd:** Ch 6, dc in same place as sl st, * ch 5, between next 2 petals make dc, ch 3 and dc. Repeat from * around, ending with ch 5. Join to 3rd ch of ch-6. **5th rnd:** Ch 3, make * 6 dc in ch-3 sp, dc in next dc, ch 5, dc in next dc. Repeat from * around. Join. **6th rnd:** Ch 3, holding back on hook the last loop of each dc, make dc in next 7 dc, thread over and draw through all loops on hook (cluster made), * ch 7, sc in next sp, ch 7, make a cluster as before over next 8 dc. Repeat from * around. Join. **7th rnd:** Sl st to center of loop, sc in same loop, * ch 7, sc in next loop. Repeat from * around. Join. **8th rnd:** Ch 4, holding back on hook the last loop of each tr make a 3-tr cluster in same place as sl st, ch 4, make another 3-tr cluster in same place as last cluster was made, * ch 7, in next sc make cluster, ch 4 and cluster. Repeat from * around. Join. **9th rnd:** Sl st to center of next sp, sc in same sp, * ch 5, in center st of next chain make dc, ch 3 and dc (shell made); ch 5, sc in next sp. Repeat from * around. Join. **10th rnd:**

Sl st in next 2 ch, sc in next ch, * ch 3, shell in sp of next shell (shell made over shell); (ch 3, sc in center st of next ch-5) twice. Repeat from * around. Join. **11th rnd:** Sl st in next 3 ch, in next dc and in sp of shell, ch 6, dc in same sp (starting shell made over shell), * ch 3, skip ch-3 sp, 8 tr in next sp, ch 3, shell over shell. Repeat from * around. Join. **12th rnd:** Sl st in next sp, * shell over shell, ch 3, (tr in next tr, ch 1) 7 times; tr in next tr, ch 3. Repeat from * around. Join. **13th rnd:** * Shell over shell, ch 3, sc in next tr, (ch 4, sc in next tr) 7 times; ch 3. Repeat from * around. Join. **14th rnd:** * Shell over shell, ch 3, sc in ch-4 loop, (ch 4, sc in next loop) 6 times; ch 3. Repeat from * around. Join.

15th rnd: * Shell over shell, ch 3, sc in ch-4 loop, (ch 4, sc in next loop) 5 times; ch 3. Repeat from * around. Join. **16th rnd:** Sl st in next sp, ch 6, in sp of same shell make dc, ch 3 and dc (2 shells made); * ch 3, sc in ch-4 loop, (ch 4, sc in next loop) 4 times; ch 3, in sp of next shell make (dc, ch 3) twice and dc (2 shells made). Repeat from * around. Join. **17th rnd:** * Shell over shell, ch 3, shell over next shell, ch 3, sc in next loop, (ch 4, sc in next loop) 3 times; ch 3. Repeat from * around. Join. **18th rnd:** * Shell over shell, ch 1, shell in next sp, ch 1, shell over shell, ch 3, sc in next ch-4

loop, (ch 4, sc in next loop) twice; ch 3. Repeat from * around. Join. **19th rnd:** * (Shell over shell, ch 3) 3 times; sc in ch-4 loop, ch 4, sc in next loop, ch 3. Repeat from * around. Join. **20th rnd:** * (Shell over shell, ch 3, dc in next sp, ch 3) twice; shell over shell, ch 3, sc in next ch-4 loop, ch 3. Repeat from * around. Join. **21st rnd:** * Shell over shell, ** (ch 3, dc in next sp) twice; ch 3. Repeat from ** once more, (shell over shell) twice. Repeat from ** around. Join. **22nd rnd:** Sl st in next sp, ch 4 (to count as tr), and complete a 3-tr cluster in same sp, * ch 6, skip next sp, (make a 3-tr cluster in next dc) twice; ch 6, shell over shell, ch 6, skip next sp, (cluster in next dc) twice; ch 6, (cluster in sp of next shell) twice. Repeat from * around. Join. **23rd rnd:** Ch 4, and complete a cluster in same place as sl st, (ch 5, cluster in tip of next cluster) twice; * ch 5, shell over shell, (ch 5, cluster in tip of next cluster) 6 times. Repeat from * around. Join. **24th rnd:** Sl st to center of next sp, sc in same sp, * ch 4, in next sp make dc, ch 3 and dc; ch 4, sc in next sp, ch 4, shell over shell, ch 4, sc in next sp. Repeat from * around. Join. **25th rnd:** Sl st in next 2 ch, sc in same loop, * ch 4, shell over shell, ch 4, sc in next sp, ch 3, sc in next sp. Repeat from * around. Join and break off.

Pineapple Runner

Directions on page 9.

Pineapple Vanity Set

Pineapple Runner & Vanity Set

RUNNER

Illustrated on page 7.

MATERIALS: J. & P. Coats or Clark's O.N.T. Best Six Cord Mercerized Crochet, *Size 30:* **Small Ball:** J. & P. Coats—*3 balls of White or Ecru, or 4 balls of any color, or* Clark's O.N.T.—*4 balls of White or Ecru, or 5 balls of any color . . . Steel Crochet Hook No. 10.*

Runner measures 12 x 30 inches

PINEAPPLE MOTIF (Make 8)—Round Motif . . . Starting at center, ch 12. Join with sl st to form ring. **1st rnd:** Ch 3, 23 dc in ring. Join. **2nd rnd:** Ch 4, * dc in next dc, ch 1. Repeat from * around. Join last ch-1 to 3rd st of ch-4 (24 sps). **3rd rnd:**

Sc in sp, * ch 5, sc in next sp. Repeat from * around, ending with ch 2, dc in 1st sc (24 loops). **4th and 5th rnds:** * Ch 5, sc in next loop. Repeat from * around, ending with ch 2, dc in dc. **6th rnd:** * Ch 6, sc in next loop. Repeat from * around, ending with ch 3, dc in dc. **7th rnd:** * Ch 7, sc in next loop. Repeat from * around, ending with ch 3, tr in dc.

First Pineapple . . . 1st row: Ch 3, in last loop make dc, ch 2 and 2 dc (shell made), ch 1, in next loop make 2 dc, ch 5 and 2 dc; ch 1, in next loop make 2 dc, ch 2 and 2 dc (another shell made). Ch 5, turn. **2nd row:** Shell in sp of shell, ch 1, 15 tr in next ch-5 sp, ch 1, shell over shell. Ch 5, turn. **3rd row:** Shell over shell, ch 1, (tr in next tr, ch 1) 14 times; tr in next tr, ch 1, shell over shell. Ch 5, turn. **4th row:** Shell over shell, ch 4, skip next ch-1 sp, sc in next ch-1 sp, (ch 3, sc in next sp) 13 times; ch 4, shell over shell. Ch 5, turn. **5th row:** Shell over shell, ch 4, sc in next ch-3 loop, (ch 3, sc in next loop) 12 times; ch 4, shell over shell. Ch 5, turn. Continue in this manner until 1 loop remains. **Next row:** Shell over shell, ch 4, sc in ch-3 loop, ch 4, 2 dc in sp of next shell, ch 1, sl st in sp of last shell made, ch 1, 2 dc in same place as last 2 dc were made, ch 5, turn, sl st in joining of shells. Break off.

Second Pineapple . . . With right side facing, skip 9 loops on Round Motif, attach thread to next loop, ch 3, in same loop make dc, ch 2 and 2 dc, ch 1, in next loop make 2 dc, ch 5 and 2 dc; ch 1, shell in next loop. Ch 5, turn. Complete as for other pineapple. This completes one Pineapple Motif.

Place motifs side by side and sew the center free loops of the adjacent Round Motifs together.

Work 2 more pineapples on the 2 Round Motifs at each end, leaving 1 loop free between pineapples.

EDGING . . . 1st rnd: With right side facing, attach thread to 3rd loop from base of any pineapple, * (ch 7, sc in next loop) 11 times; ch 5, sc in 3rd loop from base of next pineapple. Repeat from * around. Join last ch-5 to base of first ch-7. **2nd rnd:** Sl st to center of next loop, sc in loop, * (ch 8, sc in next loop) 10 times; ch 2, skip ch-5, sc in next loop. Repeat from * around. Join. **3rd rnd:** Sl st to center of next loop, sc in loop, (ch 9, sc in next loop) 9 times; * sc in next ch-8 loop, ch 4, sl st in last ch-9 loop, ch 4, sc in next ch-8 loop, (ch 9, sc in next loop) 8 times. Repeat from * around, ending with ch 4, sl st in first ch-9 loop, ch 4, sc in next ch-8 loop of last rnd. Join and break off. **4th rnd:** Attach thread to next free ch-9 loop, sc in same loop, * (ch 10, sc in next loop) twice; ch 10, in next loop make (cluster, ch 10) twice and clus-

ter—to make a cluster, holding back on hook the last loop of each tr make 3 tr in same loop, thread over and draw through all loops on hook; (ch 10, sc in next loop) 3 times; ch 10, sc in next free ch-9 loop. Repeat from * around. Join. **5th rnd:** Sl st to center of next loop, sc in loop, * (ch 10, sc in next loop) 7 times; ch 3, sc in next loop, ch 3, sc in next loop. Repeat from * around, making ch 10 (instead of ch-3) between pineapples at curved ends. Join. **6th rnd:** Sl st to center of next loop, (ch 10, sc in next loop) 6 times; ch 5, sc in next ch-10 loop, ch 10 and continue thus around, making sc, ch 5 and sc over each joining between pineapples. **7th rnd:** Make ch-10 loops around, having ch 5 over each ch-5 across long sides and ch 10 over each ch-5 at curved ends. Join and break off.

FILL-IN MOTIF . . . Starting at center, ch 10. Join with sl st to form ring. **1st rnd:** Sc in ring, (ch 5, sc in ring) 11 times; ch 2, dc in 1st sc. **2nd rnd:** (Ch 5, sc in next loop) 11 times; ch 2, dc in dc. **3rd rnd:** * Ch 2, sl st in 2nd free loop on Round Motif, ch 2, sc in next loop on Fill-in-Motif, ch 2, sc in next loop on Round Motif, ch 2, sc in next loop on Fill-in-Motif, ch 5, sc in next loop. Repeat from * 3 more times, joining 2 loops to next Round Motif as before and 2 loops to 2nd and 3rd free loops on each pineapple. Join last ch-5 to base of first ch-2. Fill in all other spaces in the same way (14 in all).

VANITY SET

MATERIALS: J. & P. Coats or Clark's O.N.T. Best Six Cord Mercerized Crochet, *Size 30:* **Small Ball:** J. & P. Coats—*4 balls of White or Ecru, or 5 balls of any color, or* Clark's O.N.T.—*5 balls of White or Ecru, or 6 balls of any color.* **Big Ball:** J. & P. Coats—*2 balls of White, Ecru or Cream . . . Steel Crochet Hook No. 10.*

Oval Doily measures 12 x 17 inches; Round Doily 12 inches in diameter

OVAL DOILY . . . Make 3 Pineapple Motifs as for the Runner and join. Work 2 more pineapples on the 2 Round Motifs at each end, leaving 1 loop free between pineapples. Complete as for Runner.

ROUND DOILY (Make 2) . . . Make 1 Pineapple Motif as for Oval Doily. Work 2 more pineapples on the Round Motif on each side, leaving 1 loop free between pineapples. Complete as for Oval Doily, omitting Fill-in-Motifs and working Edging between pineapples to correspond with curved ends of Oval Doily.

Pineapple Fan

Chair Back measures 10½ x 20 inches
Arm pieces measure 7½ x 10½ inches each

MATERIALS:

J. & P. Coats or Clark's O.N.T. Best Six Cord Mercerized Crochet, Size 30:

SMALL BALL:

J. & P. COATS—6 balls of White or Ecru, or 8 balls of any color, or

CLARK'S O.N.T.—8 balls of White or Ecru, or 10 balls of any color, or

BIG BALL:

J. & P. COATS—4 balls of White or Ecru, or 5 balls of any color, or

Clark's Big Ball Three Cord Mercerized Crochet, Size 30: 3 balls of White or Ecru, or 4 balls of any color.

Milward's Steel Crochet Hook No. 10.

CHAIR BACK . . . Starting at top, ch 35. **1st row:** Sc in 7th ch from hook, * ch 3, skip 3 ch, sc in next ch. Repeat from * across (8 sps). Ch 7, turn. **2nd row:** Holding back on hook the last loop of each tr make 2 tr in first sp, thread over and draw through all loops on hook (cluster made); * (ch 2, cluster in same sp) twice; ch 2, cluster in next sp. Repeat from * across. Ch 7, turn. **3rd row:** Cluster in first cluster, * (ch 2, cluster in next cluster) twice; ch 4, cluster in next cluster. Repeat from * across. Ch 7, turn. **4th row:** Cluster in first cluster, * (ch 2, cluster in next cluster) twice; ch 6, cluster in next cluster. Repeat from * across. Ch 7, turn. **5th row:** Cluster in first cluster, * (ch 3, cluster in next cluster) twice; ch 6, cluster in next cluster. Repeat from * across. Ch 7, turn. **6th row:** Cluster in first cluster, * (ch 3, cluster in next cluster) twice; ch 7, cluster in next cluster. Repeat from * across. Ch 7, turn. **7th row:** Cluster in first cluster, * (ch 4, cluster in next cluster) twice; ch 7, cluster in next cluster. Repeat from * across. Ch 7, turn. **8th row:** Cluster in first cluster, * (ch 4, cluster in next cluster) twice; ch 8, cluster in next cluster. Repeat from * across. Ch 7, turn. **9th row:** Cluster in first cluster, * (ch 5, cluster in next cluster) twice; ch 8, cluster in next cluster. Repeat from * across. Ch 7, turn.

10th row: Cluster in first cluster, * (ch 5, cluster in next cluster) twice; ch 9, cluster in next cluster. Repeat from * across. Ch 7, turn. **11th row:** Cluster in first cluster, * (ch 5, cluster in next cluster) twice; ch 10, cluster in next cluster. Repeat from * across. Ch 7, turn. **12th row:** Cluster in first cluster, * (ch 5, cluster in next cluster) twice; ch 5, cluster in next sp, ch 5, cluster in next cluster. Repeat from * across. Ch 7, turn. **13th row:**

Cluster in first cluster, * (ch 5, cluster in next cluster) twice; ch 4, in next cluster make cluster, ch 2 and cluster; ch 4, cluster in next cluster. Repeat from * across. Ch 7, turn. **14th row:** Cluster in first cluster, * (ch 5, cluster in next cluster) 3 times; ch 3, cluster in next cluster, ch 5, cluster in next cluster. Repeat from * across. Ch 7, turn. **15th row:** Cluster in first cluster, * (ch 5, cluster in next cluster) twice; ch 6, cluster in next cluster, ch 3, cluster in next cluster, ch 6, cluster in next cluster. Repeat from * across. Ch 7, turn. **16th row:** Cluster in first cluster, * (ch 5, cluster in next cluster) twice; ch 7, cluster in next cluster, ch 3, cluster in next cluster, ch 7, cluster in next cluster. Repeat from * across. Ch 7, turn. **17th row:** Cluster in first cluster, * (ch 5, cluster in next cluster) twice; ch 8, cluster in next cluster, ch 3, cluster in next cluster, ch 8, cluster in next cluster. Repeat from * across. Ch 7, turn. **18th row:** Cluster in first cluster, * (ch 5, cluster in next cluster) twice; ch 9, cluster in next cluster, ch 3, cluster in next cluster, ch 9, cluster in next cluster. Repeat from * across. Ch 7, turn. **19th row:** Cluster in first cluster, * ch 5, in next cluster make cluster, ch 5 and cluster; ch 5, cluster in next cluster, ch 8, cluster in next cluster, ch 3, cluster in next cluster, ch 8, cluster in next cluster. Repeat from * across. Ch 7, turn.

20th row: Cluster in first cluster, * ch 2, skip next sp, 13 tr in next sp, ch 2, skip next sp, cluster in next cluster, ch 7, cluster in next cluster, ch 3, cluster in next cluster, ch 7, cluster in next cluster. Repeat from * across. Ch 7, turn. **21st row:** Cluster in first cluster, * ch 1, (tr in next tr, ch 1) 13 times; cluster in next cluster, ch 6, cluster in next cluster, ch 3, cluster in next cluster, ch 6, cluster in next cluster. Repeat from * across. Ch 7, turn. **22nd row:** Cluster in first cluster, * ch 3, skip 1 sp, (sc in next sp, ch 3) 11 times; sc in next sp, (ch 3, cluster in next cluster, ch 5, cluster in next cluster) twice. Repeat from * across. Ch 7, turn. **23rd row:** Cluster in first cluster, * ch 3, skip next sp, 3 dc in each of next 11 loops, (ch 3, cluster in next cluster, ch 4, cluster in next cluster) twice. Repeat from * across. Ch 7, turn. **24th row:** Cluster in first cluster, * ch 3, holding back on hook the last loop of each dc make dc in next 3 dc, thread over and draw through all loops on hook (2 dc decreased), dc in each dc across to within last 3 dc, dec 2 dc as before, (ch 3, cluster in next cluster, ch 4, cluster in next cluster) twice. Repeat from * across. Ch 7, turn. **25th row:** Cluster in first cluster, * ch 3, dec 2 dc, dc in

each dc across to within last 3 dc, dec 2 dc, ch 3, (cluster in next cluster, ch 4) twice; cluster in next sp, (ch 4, cluster in next cluster) twice. Repeat from * across. Ch 7, turn. **26th row:** Cluster in first cluster, * ch 3, dec 2 dc, dc in each dc across to within last 3 dc, dec 2 dc, ch 3, (cluster in next cluster, ch 4) twice; in next cluster make cluster, ch 5 and cluster; (ch 4, cluster in next cluster) twice. Repeat from * across. Ch 7, turn. **27th row:** Cluster in first cluster, * ch 3, dec 2 dc, dc in each dc across to within last 3 dc, dec 2 dc, ch 3, cluster in next cluster, ch 4, cluster in next cluster, ch 3, skip next sp, 13 tr in next sp, ch 3, skip next sp, cluster in next cluster, ch 4, cluster in next cluster. Repeat from * across. Ch 7, turn.

28th row: Cluster in first cluster, * ch 3, dec 2 dc, dc in each dc across to within last 3 dc, dec 2 dc, ch 3, cluster in next cluster, ch 4, cluster in next cluster, ch 1, (tr in next tr, ch 1) 13 times; ch 1, cluster in next cluster, ch 4, cluster in next cluster. Repeat from * across. Ch 7, turn. **29th row:** Cluster in first cluster, * ch 3, dec 2 dc, dc in each dc across to within last 3 dc, dec 2 dc, ch 3, cluster in next cluster, ch 4, cluster in next cluster, ch 3, skip next sp, (sc in next sp, ch 3) 11 times; sc in next sp, ch 3, cluster in next cluster, ch 4, cluster in next cluster. Repeat from * across. Ch 7, turn. **30th row:** Cluster in first cluster, * ch 3, dec 2 dc, dc in each dc across to within last 3 dc, dec 2 dc, ch 3, cluster in next cluster, ch 4, cluster in next cluster, ch 3, skip next sp, 3 dc in each of next 11 loops, ch 3, cluster in next cluster, ch 4, cluster in next cluster. Repeat from * across. Ch 7, turn. **31st row:** Cluster in first cluster, * ch 3, make a 5-tr cluster over next 5 dc, ch 3, cluster in next cluster, ch 4, cluster in next cluster, ch 3, dec 2 dc, dc in each dc across to within last 3 dc, dec 2 dc, ch 3, cluster in next cluster, ch 4, cluster in next cluster. Repeat from * across. Ch 7, turn. **32nd row:** Holding back on hook the last loop of each tr make 2 tr in each of next 2 clusters, thread over and draw through all loops on hook (joint cluster made), ch 6, cluster in next cluster, * ch 3, dec 2 dc, dc in each dc across to within last 3 dc, dec 2 dc, ch 3, cluster in next cluster, ch 6, make a joint cluster over next 2 clusters, ch 6, cluster in next cluster. Repeat from * across. Ch 7, turn.

33rd row: * In tip of joint cluster make cluster, ch 5 and cluster; ch 4, cluster in next cluster, ch 3, dec 2 dc,. dc in each dc across to within last 3 dc, dec 2 dc, ch 3, cluster in next cluster, ch 4. Repeat from * across. Ch 7, turn. **34th row:** * 13 tr in next

sp, ch 5, cluster in next cluster, ch 3, dec 2 dc, dc in each dc across to within last 3 dc, dec 2 dc, ch 3, cluster in next cluster, ch 5. Repeat from * across. Ch 7, turn. **35th row:** Tr in first tr, * (ch 1, tr in next tr) 12 times; ch 3, cluster in next cluster, ch 3, dec 2 dc, dc in each dc across to within last 3 dc, dec 2 dc, ch 3, cluster in next cluster, ch 3, tr in next tr. Repeat from * across. Ch 7, turn. **36th row:** * (Cluster in next ch-1 sp, ch 2) 11 times; cluster in next sp, ch 3, cluster in next cluster, ch 3, dec 2 dc, dc in each dc across

to within last 3 dc, dec 2 dc, ch 3, cluster in next cluster, ch 3. Repeat from * across. Break off and turn.
Now work points of pineapples individually as follows: **1st row:** Skip 12 clusters, attach thread to next cluster, ch 7, cluster in same place, ch 3, dec 2 dc, dc in each dc across to within last 3 dc, dec 2 dc, ch 3, cluster in next cluster. Ch 7, turn. **2nd row:** Cluster in first cluster, ch 3, make a 5-tr cluster over next 5 dc, ch 3, cluster in next cluster. Ch 7, turn. **3rd row:** Make a joint cluster over next 2 clus-

ters. Break off. Complete other pineapples the same way.

EDGING . . . Attach thread to 11th ch-7 loop along side, sc in same place, * ch 1, in next loop make (3-tr cluster, ch 5) 3 times and 3-tr cluster; ch 1, sc in next loop. Repeat from * along side, across top and along opposite side to correspond. Break off.

ARM PIECE (Make 2) . . . Starting at top, ch 15. Complete as for Chair Back. Starch lightly and press.

11

Pineapple Doily & Apron

DOILY

MATERIALS: J. & P. Coats or Clark's O.N.T. Best Six Cord Mercerized Crochet, Size 30: **Small Ball:** J. & P. Coats—2 balls of *White, Ecru or color,* or Clark's O.N.T.—3 balls of *White, Ecru or color . . . Steel Crochet Hook No. 10 . . . A piece of linen 5½ inches in diameter.*

Doily measures 15½ inches in diameter.

CENTER . . . Make a narrow hem around edge of linen and work sc evenly around, keeping edge flat. Join and break off.

INSERTION . . . Ch 15. **1st row:** In 6th ch from hook make 2 dc, ch 2 and 2 dc (shell made); ch 5, skip 8 ch, in next ch make 2 dc, ch 2 and 2 dc (another shell made). Ch 5, turn. **2nd row:** Shell in sp of shell, ch 3, sc in next sp, ch 5, shell over shell. Ch 5, turn. **3rd row:** (Shell over shell, ch 5) twice. Turn. Repeat the 2nd and 3rd rows alternately until there are 56 turning ch-5 loops on one side.

Place 1st and last rows of Insertion together and join with sl st to form a circle, having the 56 loops on outer edge. Work around inner edge as follows: Sl st to center of first ch-5 loop, sc in same loop, * ch 3, sc in next loop. Repeat from * around. Join and break off. Sew this rnd to edge of linen center.

PINEAPPLE BORDER . . . 1st rnd: Attach thread to first ch-5 loop on Insertion, ch 3, in same loop make dc, ch 2 and 2 dc; in next loop make 2 dc, ch 2 and 2 dc (shell made); * (ch 3, shell in next loop) 3 times; (ch 3, shell in next 2 loops) twice. Repeat from * around, ending with ch 3, sl st in top of starting chain. **2nd rnd:** Sl st in next dc and in sp, ch 3, in same sp make dc, ch 2 and 2 dc (shell made over shell), shell over next shell, * (ch 3, shell over shell) 4 times; shell over shell, ch 3, sc in next sp, ch 3, shell over next 2 shells. Repeat from * around. Join. **3rd rnd:** * (Shell over shell) twice; (ch 3, shell over shell) 4 times; shell over shell, ch 5. Repeat from * around. Join. **4th rnd:** Repeat 2nd rnd. **5th rnd:** * (Shell over shell) twice; ch 3, shell over shell, ch 3, in sp of next shell make 2 dc, ch 5 and 2 dc; (ch 3, shell over shell) twice; shell over shell, ch 5. Repeat from * around. Join. **6th rnd:** * (Shell over shell) twice; ch 3, shell over shell, 15 tr in next ch-5 sp, shell over shell, ch 3, (shell over shell) twice; ch 3, sc in next sp, ch 3. Repeat from * around. Join. **7th rnd:** * (Shell over shell) twice; ch 3, shell over shell, (tr in next tr, ch 1) 14 times; tr in next tr, shell over shell, ch 3, (shell over shell) twice; ch 5. Repeat from * around. Join. **8th rnd:** * (Shell over shell) twice; ch 3, shell over shell, ch 4, sc in next ch-1 sp, (ch 3, sc in next sp) 13 times; ch 4, shell over shell, ch 3, (shell over shell) twice; ch 3, sc in next sp, ch 3. Repeat from * around. Join. **9th rnd:** * (Shell over shell) twice; ch 3, shell over shell, ch 4, sc in next ch-3 loop, (ch 3, sc in next loop) 12 times; ch 4, shell over shell, ch 3, (shell over shell) twice; ch 5. Repeat from * around. Join. **10th rnd:** * (Shell over shell) twice; ch 3, shell over shell, ch 4, sc in next ch-3 loop, (ch 3, sc in next loop) 11 times; ch 4, shell over shell, ch 3, (shell over shell) twice; ch 3, sc in next sp, ch 3. Repeat from * around. Join.

FIRST PINEAPPLE . . . 1st row: (Shell over shell) twice; ch 3, shell over shell, ch 4, sc in next ch-3 loop, (ch 3, sc in next loop) 10 times; ch 4, shell over shell, ch 3, shell in next 2 shells. Ch 5, turn. **2nd row:** (Shell over shell) twice; ch 3, shell over shell, ch 4, sc in next ch-3 loop, (ch 3, sc in next loop) 9 times; ch 4, shell over shell, ch 3, shell in next 2 shells. Ch 5, turn. **3rd to 10th rows incl:** Work in this manner, having 1 loop less on each row until 1 loop remains on 10th row. Ch 5, turn. **11th row:** (Shell over shell) twice; ch 3, shell over shell, ch 4, sc in ch-3 loop, ch 4, shell over shell, ch 3, (shell over shell) twice. Ch 5, turn. **12th row:** (Shell over shell) twice; ch 1, 2 dc in next 2 shells, ch 1, (shell over shell) twice. Ch 5, turn. **13th row:** (Shell over shell) 4 times. Ch 5, turn. **14th row:** Shell over shell, 2 dc in next 2 shells, shell over shell. Ch 5, turn. **15th row:** Shell over shell, 2 dc in sp of next shell, ch 1, sl st in sp of last shell, ch 1, 2 dc where last 2 dc were made. Ch 5, turn and sl st in joining of shells. Break off.

SECOND PINEAPPLE . . . Attach thread to sp of next shell, ch 5, and work to correspond with First Pineapple. Complete other pineapples to correspond.

APRON

MATERIALS: J. & P. Coats or Clark's O.N.T. Best Six Cord Mercerized Crochet, Size 30: **Small Ball:** J. & P. Coats—5 balls of *White or Ecru,* or 6 balls of any color, or Clark's O.N.T.—7 balls of *White or Ecru,* or 9 balls of any color. **Big Ball:** J. & P. Coats—3 balls of *White, Ecru or Cream . . . Steel Crochet Hook No. 10 . . . 3 yards of ribbon, ¼ inch* wide . . . 1½ *yards of ribbon, 1 inch wide.*

WAISTBAND . . . Work exactly as for Insertion for Doily until there are 42 turning ch-5 loops on one long side. Break off.

SKIRT . . . 1st row: Working along edge with 42 loops, attach thread to 1st loop, ch 3, in same loop make dc, ch 2 and 2 dc; in next loop make 2 dc, ch 2 and 2 dc (shell made), * (ch 3, shell in next loop) 3 times; (ch 3, shell in next 2 loops) twice. Repeat from * across, ending with ch 3, shell in next 2 loops. Ch 5, turn. **2nd row:** * (Shell over shell) twice; (ch 3, shell over shell) 4 times; shell over shell, ch 3, sc in next sp, ch 3. Repeat from * across. Ch 5, turn. **3rd row:** * (Shell over shell) twice; (ch 3, shell over shell) 4 times; shell over shell, ch 5. Repeat from * across. Ch 5, turn. Repeat the 2nd and 3rd rows alternately until Skirt measures 15 inches, ending with the 2nd row. Ch 5, turn.

PINEAPPLE BORDER . . . 1st row: * (Shell over shell) twice; ch 3, shell over shell, ch 3, in sp of next shell make 2 dc, ch 5 and 2 dc; (ch 3, shell over shell) twice; shell over shell, ch 5. Repeat from * across. Ch 5, turn. **2nd row:** * (Shell over shell) twice; ch 3, shell over shell, 15 tr in next ch-5 sp, shell over shell, ch 3, (shell over shell) twice; ch 3, sc in next sp, ch 3. Repeat from * across. Ch 5, turn. **3rd row:** * (Shell over shell) twice; ch 3, shell over shell, (tr in next tr, ch 1) 14 times; tr in next tr, shell over shell, ch 3, (shell over shell) twice; ch 5. Repeat from * across. Ch 5, turn. **4th row:** * (Shell over shell) twice; ch 3, shell over shell, ch 4, sc in next ch-1 sp, (ch 3, sc in next sp) 13 times; ch 4, shell over shell, ch 3, shell in next 2 shells, ch 3, sc in next sp, ch 3. Repeat from * across. Ch 5, turn. **5th row:** * (Shell over shell) twice; ch 3, shell over shell, ch 4, skip next ch-4, sc in next ch-3 loop, (ch 3, sc in next loop) 12 times; ch 4, shell over shell, ch 3, shell in next 2 shells, ch 5. Repeat from * across. Ch 5, turn. **6th row:** * (Shell over shell) twice; ch 3, shell over shell, ch 4, sc in next ch-3 loop, (ch 3, sc in next loop) 11 times; ch 4, shell over shell, ch 3, shell in next 2 shells; ch 3, sc in next sp, ch 3. Repeat from * across. Ch 5, turn.

Starting at First Pineapple, complete pineapples as for the Doily. Run narrow ribbon through rows of Skirt between pineapples and through waistband. Sew ends in place. Cut remainder of narrow ribbon into 5 equal parts and tie in bows. Sew a bow at bottom of each ribbon. Cut wide ribbon in half and sew to Waistband for ties.

Pineapple Bedspread or Tablecloth

BEDSPREAD or TABLECLOTH
90 x 108 inches

MATERIALS: J. & P. Coats Big Ball Best Six Cord Mercerized Crochet, *Size 30: 78 balls of White, Ecru or Cream*, or Clark's O.N.T. Big Ball Three Cord Mercerized Crochet, *Size 30: 63 balls of White, Ecru or Cream . . . Steel Crochet Hook No. 10.*

TABLECLOTH
65 x 84 inches

MATERIALS: J. & P. Coats Big Ball Best Six Cord Mercerized Crochet, *Size 30: 68 balls of White, Ecru or Cream*, or Clark's Big Ball Three Cord Mercerized Crochet, *Size 30: 56 balls of White, Ecru or Cream . . . Steel Crochet Hook No. 10.*

GAUGE: 3 shells and 3 ch-6 sps make 2 inches; 5 rows of shells make 1 inch. Starting at center, make a chain about 25 inches long (13 ch sts to 1 inch). **1st rnd:** In 4th ch from hook make dc, ch 2 and 2 dc (shell made); * ch 6, skip 10 ch, in next ch make 2 dc, ch 2 and 2 dc (another shell made). Repeat from * across until 29 shells are complete. Cut off remaining chain, ch 6 and, working along opposite side of starting chain, ** make a shell at base of next shell, ch 6. Repeat from ** across, ending with ch 6, sl st in top of turning chain. **2nd rnd:** Sl st in next dc and in sp, ch 3, in same sp make dc, ch 2 and 2 dc; * ch 6, shell in sp of next shell (shell over shell made). Repeat from * across one side, ch 2, in end ch-6 sp make 2 dc, ch 3, 2 dc (corner shell made), ch 2; in same sp make 2 dc, ch 3 and 2 dc (another corner shell made); ch 2, shell in sp of next shell, ch 6 and work across other side to correspond. Make end as before. Join. **3rd rnd:** Sl st in next dc and in next sp, in same sp make dc, ch 2 and 2 dc —each rnd begins in this way and this will be referred to as shell over shell. Ch 6 and shell over shell alternately across to corner, ch 3, shell over corner shell, ch 3, shell in sp between shells, ch 3, shell in next corner shell, ch 3 and work remainder of rnd to correspond. Join. **4th rnd:** * Shell over shell, ch 6. Repeat from * to corner;

Continued on page 16.

14

BEDSPREAD or TABLECLOTH

Continued from page 14.

(ch 4, shell in next shell) 3 times; ch 4 and work remainder of rnd to correspond. Join. **5th rnd:** * Shell over shell, ch 6. Repeat from * around. Join. **6th rnd:** * Shell over shell, ch 6. Repeat from * across to corner shell; in corner shell make shell, ch 3 and shell; ch 6, shell over shell, ch 6, in corner shell make shell, ch 3 and shell. Complete rnd to correspond. Join. **7th rnd:** Work as for last rnd to corner, ch 6, shell over shell, ch 2, shell in ch-3 sp (between shells), ch 2, shell over shell, ch 6 and continue as before, making all corners to correspond. Join. **8th rnd:** Work as before to corner, ch 6, (shell over shell, ch 1, shell in sp between shells, ch 1) twice; shell over shell (5 shells in corner). Ch 6 and work as before, making all corners to correspond. Join. **9th rnd:** Work as before to corner, ch 6, shell over corner shell, (ch 3, shell over shell) 4 times; ch 6 and work as before, making all corners to correspond. Join. **10th rnd:** Repeat 9th rnd, making ch 4 over each ch-3 sp. Join. **11th rnd:** Repeat 10th rnd, making ch 5 over each ch-4 sp. Join. Repeat 6th to 11th rnds incl 5 more times (41 rnds completed).

42nd rnd: Sl st in next dc and in next sp, ch 3, in same sp make dc, ch 7 and 2 dc; * (ch 6, shell over shell) 3 times; ch 6, in sp of next shell make 2 dc, ch 7 and 2 dc. Repeat from * 9 more times, ch 6, shell in center shell of corner, ch 6, in next shell make 2 dc, ch 7 and 2 dc; ch 6 and work in the same manner over remaining 3 sides, making all corners to correspond. Join. **43rd rnd:** Sl st in next dc and in next sp, ch 4 (to count as tr), 19 tr in same sp, * shell over shell, (ch 6, shell over shell) twice; 20 tr in ch-7 sp of next shell. Repeat from * across to corner shell, ch 2, shell in corner shell, ch 2, 20 tr in ch-7 loop and work remainder of rnd to correspond. Join (42 pineapples have been started on this rnd). **44th rnd:** Ch 5, (tr in next tr, ch 1) 18 times; tr in next tr, * dc in sp of next shell, ch 6, shell over shell, ch 6, dc in sp of next shell, (tr in next tr, ch 1) 19 times; tr in next tr. Repeat from * across to corner shell, ch 2, shell over corner shell, ch 2 and complete rnd to correspond, making corners as before. Join. **45th rnd:** Sc in next ch-1 sp, * (ch 3, sc in next ch-1 sp) 18 times; ch 6, shell over shell, ch 6, sc in next ch-1 sp. Repeat from * across to corner shell, ch 2, shell over corner shell, ch 2, sc in next ch-1 sp and complete rnd to correspond, making corners as before. Join. **46th rnd:** Sl st in next ch, sc in loop, * (ch 3, sc in next loop) 17 times; ch 5, shell over shell, ch 5, sc in next ch-3 loop. Repeat from * across to corner shell, ch 2, shell over corner shell, ch 2, sc in next ch-3 loop and complete rnd to correspond, making corners as before. Join. **47th rnd:** Sl st in next ch, sc in loop, * (ch 3, sc in next loop) 16 times; ch 4, shell over shell, ch 4, sc in next ch-3 loop. Repeat from * across to corner shell,

ch 2, shell over corner shell, ch 2, sc in next ch-3 loop on next pineapple and complete to correspond. Join. **48th rnd:** Sl st in next ch, sc in loop * (ch 3, sc in next loop) 15 times; ch 4, shell over shell, ch 4, sc in next ch-3 loop. Repeat from * across to corner shell, ch 2, shell over corner shell, ch 2, complete rnd to correspond. Join. **49th rnd:** Sl st in next ch, sc in loop, * (ch 3, sc in next loop) 14 times; ch 4, shell over shell, ch 4, sc in next ch-3 loop. Repeat from * across to corner shell, ch 2, shell over corner shell, ch 2, complete rnd to correspond. Join.

50th rnd: Sl st in next ch, sc in loop, * (ch 3, sc in next loop) 13 times; ch 4, in sp of next shell make (2 dc, ch 2) twice and 2 dc; ch 4, sc in next ch-3 loop. Repeat from * across to corner shell, ch 2, in corner shell make (2 dc, ch 2) 3 times and 2 dc; ch 2, complete rnd to correspond. Join. **51st rnd:** Sl st in next ch, sc in loop, * (ch 3, sc in next loop) 12 times; ch 4, shell in next ch-2 sp, ch 2, shell in next ch-2 sp, ch 4, sc in next ch-3 loop. Repeat from * across to corner shell, ch 2, skip next ch-2, (shell in next sp, ch 2) 3 times; sc in next ch-3 loop and complete rnd to correspond. Join. **52nd rnd:** Sl st in next ch, sc in loop, * (ch 3, sc in next loop) 11 times; ch 4, shell over shell, shell in ch-2 sp between shells, shell over shell, ch 4, sc in next ch-3 loop. Repeat from * across to corner shell, ch 2, (shell over shell, shell in next sp) twice and shell over shell; ch 2, sc in next ch-3 loop and complete rnd to correspond. Join. **53rd rnd:** Sl st in next ch, sc in loop, * (ch 3, sc in next loop) 10 times; ch 4, shell over shell, (ch 2, shell over shell) twice; ch 4, sc in next ch-3 loop. Repeat from * across to corner shell, (ch 2, shell over shell) 5 times; ch 2, sc in next ch-3 loop and complete rnd to correspond. Join. **54th rnd:** Sl st in next ch, sc in loop, * (ch 3, sc in next loop) 9 times; ch 4, shell over shell, (ch 3, shell over shell) twice; ch 4, sc in next ch-3 loop. Repeat from * across to corner shell, ch 2, (shell over shell, ch 3) 4 times and shell over shell; ch 2, sc in next ch-3 loop and complete rnd to correspond. Join. **55th rnd:** Sl st in next ch, sc in loop, * (ch 3, sc in next loop) 8 times; (ch 4, shell over shell) 3 times; ch 4, sc in next ch-3 loop. Repeat from * across to corner shell, ch 2, (shell over shell, ch 4) 4 times and shell over shell; ch 2, sc in next ch-3 loop and complete rnd to correspond. Join.

56th rnd: Sl st in next ch, sc in loop, * (ch 3, sc in next loop) 7 times; ch 4, shell over shell, ch 5, in sp of next shell make 2 dc, ch 7 and 2 dc; ch 5, shell over shell, ch 4, sc in next ch-3 loop. Repeat from * across to corner shell, ch 3, shell over shell, ch 5, in sp of next shell make 2 dc, ch 7 and 2 dc; ch 5, shell over corner shell, ch 5, in sp of next shell make 2 dc, ch 7 and 2 dc; ch 5, shell over shell, ch 3, sc in next ch-3 loop and complete rnd to correspond. Join. **57th rnd:** Sl st in next ch, sc in loop, * (ch 3, sc in next loop) 6 times; ch 4, shell over shell, ch 4, 20 tr in ch-7 loop, ch 4, shell over shell, ch 4, sc in next ch-3 loop. Repeat from *

across to corner shell, ch 4, shell over shell, ch 4, 20 tr in next ch-7 sp, ch 2, shell over shell, ch 2, 20 tr in next ch-7 sp, ch 4, shell over shell, ch 4, sc in next ch-3 loop and complete rnd to correspond. Join. **58th rnd:** Sl st in next ch, sc in loop, * (ch 3, sc in next loop) 5 times; ch 4, shell over shell, ch 4, (tr in next tr, ch 1) 19 times and tr; ch 4, shell over shell, ch 4, sc in next ch-3 loop. Repeat from * across to corner shell, ch 2, shell over corner shell, ch 2, complete rnd to correspond. Join. **59th rnd:** Sl st in next ch, sc in loop, * (ch 3, sc in next loop) 4 times; ch 4, shell over shell, ch 4, sc in next ch-1 sp, (ch 3, sc in next ch-1 sp) 18 times; ch 4, shell over shell, ch 4, sc in next ch-3 loop. Repeat from * across to corner shell, ch 2, shell over shell, ch 2, sc in next ch-1 sp and complete rnd to correspond. Join. **60th rnd:** Sl st in next ch, sc in loop, * (ch 3, sc in next loop) 3 times; ch 4, shell over shell, ch 4, sc in next ch-3 loop, (ch 3, sc in next loop) 17 times; ch 4, shell over shell, ch 4, sc in next ch-3 loop. Repeat from * around, working over corners in established pattern and ending rnd as before. **61st rnd:** Sl st in next ch, sc in loop, * (ch 3, sc in next loop) twice; ch 4, shell over shell, ch 4, sc in next ch-3 loop, (ch 3, sc in next loop) 16 times; ch 4, shell over shell, ch 4, sc in next ch-3 loop. Repeat from * around, working over corners in established pattern. Join. **62nd rnd:** Sl st in next ch, sc in loop, * ch 3, sc in next loop, ch 4, shell over shell, ch 4, sc in next ch-3 loop, (ch 3, sc in next loop) 15 times; ch 4, shell over shell, ch 4, sc in next ch-3 loop. Repeat from * around, working over corners in established pattern. Join.

Note: Increases at corners are always worked in the same manner. Work over corners in pattern as established.

63rd rnd: Sl st in next ch, sc in loop, * ch 4, shell over shell, ch 4, sc in next ch-3 loop, (ch 3, sc in next loop) 14 times; ch 4, shell over shell, ch 4, sc in next ch-3 loop. Repeat from * around. Join. **64th rnd:** Sl st in next 4 ch and the following 2 dc, sl st in sp of shell, ch 3 (to count as dc), in same sp make dc, ch 2 and 2 dc; * ch 4, sc in next ch-3 loop, (ch 3, sc in next loop) 13 times; ch 4, shell over shell, ch 1, shell over shell. Repeat from * around, ending with ch 1. Join. **65th rnd:** Shell over shell, * ch 4, sc in next ch-3 loop, (ch 3, sc in next loop) 12 times; ch 4, shell over shell, shell in next ch-1, shell over shell. Repeat from * around, ending with shell in last ch-1. Join. **66th rnd:** * Shell over shell, ch 4, sc in next ch-3 loop, (ch 3, sc in next loop) 11 times, ch 4, (shell over shell, ch 1) twice. Repeat from * around. Join. **67th rnd:** * Shell over shell, ch 4, sc in next ch-3 loop, (ch 3, sc in next loop) 10 times; ch 4, (shell over shell, ch 2) twice. Repeat from * around. Join. **68th rnd:** Same as previous rnd, making 9 loops over pineapples and ch-3 (instead of ch-2) between shells. **69th rnd:** Same as previous rnd, making 8 loops over pineapples and ch-4 between shells.

70th rnd: * Shell over shell, ch 4, make 7 loops over pineapple, ch 4,

16

shell over shell, ch 5, in sp of next shell, make 2 dc, ch 7 and 2 dc; ch 5. Repeat from * around. Join. **71st rnd:** * Shell over shell, ch 4, make 6 loops over pineapple, ch 4, shell over shell, ch 4, 20 tr in next ch-7 sp, ch 4. Repeat from * around. Join. **72nd rnd:** * Shell over shell, ch 4, make 5 loops over pineapple, ch 4, shell over shell, ch 4, (tr in next tr, ch 1) 19 times and tr; ch 4. Repeat from * around. Join. **73rd rnd:** * Shell over shell, ch 4, make 4 loops over pineapple, ch 4, shell over shell, ch 4, sc in next ch-1 sp, (ch 3, sc in next ch-1 sp) 18 times; ch 4. Repeat from * around. Join. **74th rnd:** * Shell over shell, ch 4, make 3 loops over pineapple, ch 4, shell over shell, ch 4, make 17 loops over pineapple, ch 4. Repeat from * around. Join. **75th rnd:** * Shell over shell, ch 4, make 2 loops over pineapple, ch 4, shell over shell, ch 4, make 16 loops over pineapple, ch 4. Repeat from * around. Join. **76th rnd:** * Shell over shell, ch 4, make 1 loop over pineapple, ch 4, shell over shell, ch 4, make 15 loops over pineapple, ch 4. Repeat from * around. Join. **77th rnd:** * Shell over shell, ch 4,

sc in loop, ch 4, shell over shell, ch 4, make 14 loops over pineapple, ch 4. Repeat from * around. Join. **78th rnd:** * Shell over shell, ch 1, shell over shell, ch 4, make 13 loops over pineapple, ch 4. Repeat from * around. Join. **79th rnd:** * Shell over shell, shell in ch-1, shell over shell, ch 4, make 12 loops over pineapple, ch 4. Repeat from * around. Join. **80th rnd:** * (Shell over shell, ch 1) twice; shell over shell, ch 4, make 11 loops over pineapple, ch 4. Repeat from * around. Join. **81st rnd:** Same as previous rnd, making ch 2 (instead of ch-1) between shells and 10 loops over pineapples.

Continue thus in established pattern, **until 10 rnds of pineapples have been completed for Tablecloth, or 16 rnds of pineapples for Bedspread,** ending with the 78th rnd but making shell, ch 1 and shell in each corner shell on last rnd (13 loops across pineapples).

PINEAPPLES . . . 1st row: Sl st in next dc and in sp, turn, shell over shell, ch 4, 12 loops over pineapple, ch 4, shell over shell. Ch 5, turn. **2nd**

row: Shell over shell, ch 4, 11 loops over pineapple, ch 4, shell over shell. Ch 5, turn. Work in this manner, having 1 loop less over pineapple on each row until 1 loop remains. Ch 5, turn. **Next row:** Shell over shell, ch 4, sc in loop, ch 4, shell over shell. Ch 5, turn; (shell over shell) twice. Break off. Attach thread to 1st shell of next pineapple and complete in same manner. Continue thus until all pineapples are worked.

EDGING . . . 1st rnd: Attach thread in ch-1 sp between shells (at base of points), sc in same place, ch 3, * shell in turning chain of next shell, ch 2. Repeat from * around pineapple, ch 3, sc in next ch-1 sp between shells (at base of pineapples), ch 3 and continue thus around. Join. **2nd rnd:** Sl st to center of next shell, ch 5, * sc in next ch-2 sp, ch 2, in sp of next shell make dc, ch 4, sc in 4th ch from hook, and dc; ch 2. Repeat from * around pineapple, ending with dc in sp of last shell, dc in sp of 1st shell on next pineapple, ch 2, sc in next ch-2 sp, ch 2, and continue thus around. Join and break off.

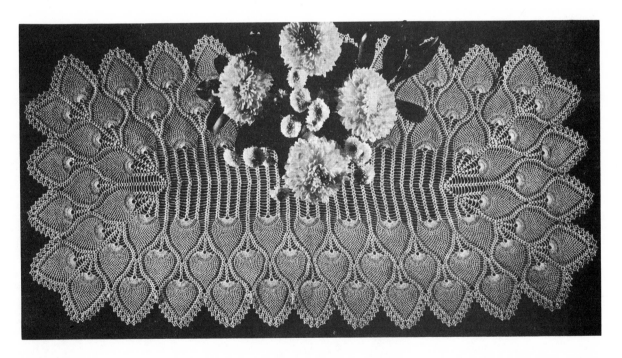

RUNNER

MATERIALS: J. & P. Coats or Clark's O.N.T. Best Six Cord Mercerized Crochet, *Size 30:* **Small Ball:** J. & P. Coats—*12 balls of White or Ecru, or 14 balls of any color,* or Clark's O.N.T.—*17 balls of White or Ecru, or 21 balls of any color.* **Big Ball:** J. & P. Coats—*7 balls of White, Ecru or Cream . . . Steel Crochet Hook No. 10.*

Runner measures 18 x 38 inches.

Work exactly as for Tablecloth until 6th rnd is completed.

7th rnd: * Shell over shell, ch 6. Repeat from * across to corner shell, (ch 6, shell over shell, ch 2, shell in next sp—this is corner shell—ch 2, shell over shell, ch 6, shell over shell) twice; ch 6 and complete rnd to correspond. Join. **8th rnd:** * Shell over shell, ch 6. Repeat from * across to corner, (ch 6, shell over shell, ch 1, shell in next sp, ch 1, shell over corner shell, ch 1, shell in next sp, ch 1, shell over shell, ch 6, shell over shell) twice. Complete rnd to correspond. Join. **9th, 10th and 11th rnds:** * Shell over shell, ch 6. Repeat from * across to corner shell, ch 6, shell over each corner shell, making ch 3 between corner shells (instead of ch-1) on 9th rnd; ch 4 (instead of ch-3) on 10th rnd and ch 5 (instead of ch-4) on

11th rnd. Break off at end of 11th rnd. **12th rnd:** Attach thread in sp of 5th shell on long side, counting from the corner shell, but do not count corner shell, ch 3, in same sp make dc, ch 7 and 2 dc; * (ch 6, shell over shell) 3 times; in next sp make 2 dc, ch 7 and 2 dc. Repeat from * 6 more times, ch 6, shell in center shell of corner, ch 6, in next shell make 2 dc, ch 7 and 2 dc. Ch 6, and work in the same manner over remaining 3 sides, making all corners to correspond. Join. **13th to 48th rnds incl:** Repeat 43rd to 78th rnds incl of Tablecloth, but on last rnd make shell, ch 1 and shell in each corner shell.

Now work Pineapples and Edging as on Tablecloth .

Pineapple Points

Doily measures 7½ inches in diameter

MATERIALS:

J. & P. Coats or **Clark's O.N.T. Best Six Cord Mercerized Crochet, Size 50:**

SMALL BALL:

J. & P. COATS—1 ball of White or Ecru, or

CLARK'S O.N.T.—2 balls of White or Ecru, or

BIG BALL:

J. & P. COATS—1 ball of White, or

Clark's Big Ball Three Cord Mercerized Crochet, Size 50: 1 ball of White.

Milward's Steel Crochet Hook No. 12.

Starting at center, ch 10. **1st rnd:** Tr in 10th ch from hook, (ch 5, tr in same ch) 6 times; ch 2, skip 3 ch, dc in next ch. **2nd rnd:** 4 sc over bar formed by dc, 7 sc in each sp around, ending with 3 sc in first sp. Join to first sc. **3rd rnd:** Ch 14, * skip 6 sc, tr in next sc, ch 10. Repeat from * around. Join to 4th ch of ch-14. **4th rnd:** Sc in same place as sl st, * 13 sc in next sp, sc in next tr. Repeat from * around. Join to first sc. **5th rnd:** Sl st in next sc, sc in same sc, sc in next 12 sc, * ch 5, skip 1 sc, sc in next 13 sc. Repeat from * around, ending with ch 2, dc in first sc. **6th rnd:** Ch 5, * sc in next 11 sc, ch 5, sc in next loop, ch 5, skip 1 sc. Repeat from * around, ending with ch 2, dc in dc. **7th rnd:** Ch 5, sc in next loop, * ch 5, skip 1 sc, sc in next 9 sc, (ch 5, sc in next loop) twice. Repeat from * around. Join as before. **8th to 11th rnds incl:** Work as for 7th rnd, having 1 loop more between sc groups and 2 sc less in each sc group on each rnd. **12th rnd:** Turn work, sl st in last sp made. Ch 1, turn. Sc in same place as sl st, * sc in next loop, (ch 5, sc in next loop) 6 times. Repeat from * around, ending with ch 2, dc in first sc. **13th rnd:** * Ch 5, sc in next loop. Repeat from * around. Join as before. **14th rnd:** * Ch 5, in next loop make tr, ch 5 and tr; (ch 5, sc in next loop) 4 times. Repeat from * around. Join as before. **15th rnd:** * Ch 5, skip next sp, 10 tr in next sp, ch 5, skip next sp, sc in next loop, (ch 5, sc in next loop) 3 times. Repeat from * around. Join as before. **16th rnd:** * Ch 5, (tr in next tr, ch 1) 9 times; tr in next tr, ch 5, skip next sp, sc in next loop, (ch 5, sc in next loop) twice. Repeat from * around. Join as before. **17th rnd:** * Ch 5, skip next sp, (sc in next sp, ch 3) 8 times; sc in next sp, ch 5, skip next sp, sc in next loop, ch 5, sc in next loop. Repeat from * around. Join as before. **18th rnd:** Sc in loop formed by ch-2 and dc, * ch 7, skip next sp, (sc in next loop, ch 3) 7 times; sc in next loop, ch 7, skip next sp, sc in next loop. Repeat from * around. Join with sl st to first sc. **19th rnd:** Ch 11, * skip next sp, (sc in next loop, ch 3) 6 times; sc in next loop, ch 7, skip next sp, in next sc make tr, ch 5 and tr; ch 7. Repeat from * around, ending with tr in first sc, ch 2,

skip 3 ch, dc in next ch. **20th rnd:** Ch 11, * skip next sp, (sc in next loop, ch 3) 5 times; sc in next loop, ch 7, skip next sp, in next sp make (tr, ch 5) twice and tr; ch 7. Repeat from * around, ending with tr, ch 5 and tr in last sp, ch 2, skip 3 ch, dc in next ch. **21st rnd:** Ch 9, tr in sp formed by ch 2 and dc, ch 5, * skip next sp, (sc in next loop, ch 3) 4 times; sc in next loop, ch 5, in each of the next 2 sps make (tr, ch 5) 3 times. Repeat from * around, ending with (tr, ch 5) twice in last sp. Join with sl st to 4th ch of ch-9.

Now work pineapples individually as follows:

FIRST PINEAPPLE . . . 1st row: Sl st in sp, ch 9, tr in same sp, ch 7, skip next sp, (sc in next loop, ch 3) 3 times; sc in next loop, ch 7, skip next sp, in next sp make tr, ch 5 and tr. Ch 9, turn. **2nd row:** Tr in first sp, ch 7, skip next sp, (sc in next loop,

ch 3) twice; sc in next loop, ch 7, skip next sp, in next sp make tr, ch 5 and tr. Ch 9, turn. **3rd row:** Tr in first sp, ch 7, skip next sp, sc in next loop, ch 3, sc in next loop, ch 7, skip next sp, in next sp make tr, ch 5 and tr. Ch 9, turn. **4th row:** Tr in first sp, ch 7, skip next sp, sc in next loop, ch 7, skip next sp, tr in next sp, ch 2, sl st in first sp, ch 2, tr in same sp as last tr. Break off.

NEXT PINEAPPLE . . . 1st row: Skip 3 sps on 21st rnd, attach thread to next sp, ch 9, tr in same sp, ch 7, skip next sp, (sc in next loop, ch 3) 3 times; sc in next loop, ch 7, skip next sp, in next sp make tr, ch 7 and tr. Ch 9, turn. Complete as for First Pineapple. Complete remaining pineapples the same way.

EDGING . . . Attach thread to first free sp on any pineapple, sc closely around. Join and break off. Starch lightly and press.

Pineapple Square Luncheon Set

SQUARE LUNCHEON SET

MATERIALS: J. & P. Coats or Clark's O.N.T. Best Six Cord Mercerized Crochet, Size 30: **Small Ball:** J. & P. Coats—10 balls of White or Ecru, or 12 balls of any color, or Clark's O.N.T.—14 balls of White or Ecru, or 18 balls of any color . . . Steel Crochet Hook No. 10.

Centerpiece measures 16½ inches square; Place Doily 13½ inches square; Bread and Butter Plate Doily 7 inches square

CENTERPIECE . . . Starting at center, ch 8. Join. **1st rnd:** Ch 3, dc in ring, ch 2, 2 dc in ring, * ch 3, in ring make 2 dc, ch 2 and 2 dc. Repeat from * 2 more times; ch 3, sl st in top of starting chain. **2nd rnd:** Sl st in next dc and in sp, ch 3, in same sp make dc, ch 2 and 2 dc (shell made

over shell), * ch 1, in next ch-3 sp make 2 dc, ch 3 and 2 dc (corner shell); ch 1, shell over shell. Repeat from * around, ending with ch 1. Join. **3rd rnd:** * Shell over shell, ch 3, corner shell over corner shell, ch 3. Repeat from * around. Join. **4th rnd:** * Shell over shell, ch 4, corner shell over corner shell, ch 4. Repeat from * around. Join. **5th rnd:** * Shell over shell, ch 6, in sp of corner shell make shell, ch 3 and shell; ch 6. Repeat from * around. Join. **6th rnd:** * Shell over shell, ch 6, shell over shell, ch 2, corner shell in next ch-3 sp, ch 2, shell over shell, ch 6. Repeat from * around. Join. **7th rnd:** * Shell over shell, ch 6, shell over shell, ch 1, shell in next sp (between shells), ch 2, corner shell over corner shell, ch 2, shell in next ch-2 sp, ch 2, shell over shell, ch 6. Repeat from * around. Join. **8th rnd:** * Shell over shell, ch 6, (shell over shell, ch 3) twice; corner shell

over corner shell, (ch 3, shell over shell) twice; ch 6. Repeat from * around. Join. **9th rnd:** * Shell over shell, ch 6, (shell over shell, ch 4) twice; corner shell over corner shell, (ch 4, shell over shell) twice; ch 6. Repeat from * around. Join. **10th rnd:** * Shell over shell, ch 6. Repeat from * around. Join. **11th rnd:** (Shell over shell, ch 6) 3 times; * in corner shell make shell, ch 3 and shell, (ch 6, shell over shell) 5 times; ch 6. Repeat from * around. Join. **12th rnd:** * Shell over shell, ch 6. Repeat from * to corner shells, shell over shell, ch 2, corner shell over next ch-3, ch 2, shell over shell, ch 6, shell over shell. Complete rnd to correspond. Join. **13th rnd:** (Shell over shell, ch 6) 3 times; shell over shell, ch 1, shell in next ch-2 sp, ch 1, corner shell over corner shell, ch 1, shell in next ch-2 sp, ch 1, shell over shell, ch 6, shell over shell.

Continued on page 20.

LUNCHEON SET

Continued from page 19.

Complete rnd to correspond. Join. **14th rnd:** (Shell over shell, ch 6) 3 times; (shell over shell, ch 3) twice; corner shell over corner shell, (ch 3, shell over shell) twice; ch 6, shell over shell, complete rnd to correspond. **15th rnd:** Same as last rnd, making ch-4 (instead of ch-3) at corners. Continue in pattern, making shell over shell and ch 6 alternately and working corners in pattern as established in 10th to 15th rnds incl (23 shells on each side on last rnd, counting corner shells). Break off.

PINEAPPLE BORDER . . . 1st rnd: Attach thread to corner shell, ch 3 and complete corner shell in same place, ** ch 3, in sp of next shell make 2 dc, ch 5 and 2 dc; ch 3, shell over shell, (ch 6, shell over shell) twice; * ch 6, in sp of next shell make 2 dc, ch 5 and 2 dc; (ch 6, shell over shell) 3 times. Repeat from * 3 more times; ch 3, in sp of next shell make 2 dc,

ch 5 and 2 dc; ch 3, corner shell in corner shell. Repeat from ** around. Join. **2nd rnd:** Sl st in next dc and in sp, ch 3, in same sp make dc, (ch 2, 2 dc) twice; * 10 tr in next ch-5 sp, shell over shell, ch 6, sc in sp of next shell, ch 6, shell over shell. Repeat from * around, making other corners to correspond. Join.

FIRST PINEAPPLE . . . 1st row: Sl st to space of second corner shell, sl st in sp, ch 3, in same sp make dc, ch 2 and 2 dc; ch 2, (tr in next tr, ch 1) 9 times; tr in next tr, ch 2, shell over shell. Ch 5, turn. **2nd row:** Shell over shell, ch 4, sc in next ch-1 sp between tr's, (ch 3, sc in next sp) 8 times; ch 4, shell over shell. Ch 5, turn. **3rd row:** Shell over shell, ch 4, sc in next ch-3 loop, (ch 3, sc in next loop) 7 times; ch 4, shell over shell. Ch 5, turn.

Work in this manner, having 1 ch-3 loop less on each row until 1 loop remains. Ch 5, turn. **Next row:** Shell over shell, ch 4, sc in next loop, ch 4, 2 dc in sp of next shell, ch 1, sl st in sp of last shell made, ch 1, 2 dc in

same place as last 2 dc were made, ch 5, turn, sl st in joining. Break off.

SECOND PINEAPPLE . . . 1st row: Attach thread in sp of next shell, ch 3, in same sp make dc, ch 2 and 2 dc; ch 2, (tr in next tr, ch 1) 9 times; tr in next tr; ch 2, shell over shell. Ch 5, turn. **2nd row:** Shell over shell, ch 4, sc in next ch-1 sp between tr's, (ch 3, sc in next sp) 8 times; ch 4, shell over shell, ch 2, sl st in corresponding ch-5 of First Pineapple. Ch 2, turn. Complete as for First Pineapple. Work all pineapples to correspond, making shell of last pineapple in first ch-2 sp of next corner but do not join corner pineapples.

PLACE DOILY (Make 2) . . . Work as for Centerpiece until 25 rnds are complete (19 shells on each side on last rnd, including corner shells). Complete as for Centerpiece.

BREAD - and - BUTTER - PLATE DOILY (Make 2) . . . Work as for Centerpiece until 8th rnd is completed. Complete as for Centerpiece (8 pineapples in all).

Pineapple Tablecloth

54 x 68 Inches

MATERIALS: J. & P. Coats Big Ball Best Six Cord Mercerized Crochet, Size 30: 26 balls of White, Ecru or Cream, or Clark's Big Ball Three Cord Mercerized Crochet, Size 30: 21 balls of White, Ecru or Cream, or 28 balls of color . . . Steel Crochet Hook No. 10.

GAUGE: Each motif measures 4½ inches square.

FIRST MOTIF . . . Starting at center, ch 10. Join with sl st to form ring. **1st rnd:** Ch 3, 23 dc in ring. Sl st in 3rd ch of ch-3. **2nd rnd:** Ch 6, * skip 1 dc, dc in next dc, ch 3. Repeat from * around. Sl st in 3rd ch of ch-6 (12 sps). **3rd rnd:** Sl st in next ch, sc in sp, (ch 7, sc in next sp) 11 times; ch 3, tr in 1st sc. **4th rnd:** Sc in loop just made, * ch 7, sc in next loop, ch 2, 12 tr in next loop, ch 2, sc in next loop. Repeat from * around. Join. **5th rnd:** Sl st in next 2 ch of ch-7 loop, ch 3, in same loop make dc, ch 2 and 2 dc (shell made), * (tr in next tr, ch 1) 11 times; tr in next tr, in next ch-7 loop make 2 dc, ch 2 and 2 dc (another shell made). Repeat from * around. Join. **6th rnd:** Sl st in next dc and in sp, ch 3, in same sp make dc, (ch 2, 2 dc) twice; * ch 4, sc in next

ch-1 sp, (ch 3, sc in next sp) 10 times; ch 4, in sp of next shell make (2 dc, ch 2) twice and 2 dc. Repeat from * around. Join. **7th rnd:** Sl st in next dc and in sp, ch 3, in same sp make dc, ch 2 and 2 dc; shell in next sp, * ch 4, sc in next ch-3 loop, (ch 3, sc in next loop) 9 times; ch 4, shell in next two ch-2 sps. Repeat from * around. Join.

FIRST PINEAPPLE . . . 1st row: Sl st across to sp of 2nd shell, ch 3, in same sp make dc, ch 2 and 2 dc; ch 4, sc in next ch-3 loop, (ch 3, sc in next loop) 8 times; ch 4, shell over shell. Ch 5, turn. **2nd row:** Shell over shell, ch 4, sc in next ch-3 loop, (ch 3, sc in next loop) 7 times; ch 4, shell over shell. Ch 5, turn.

Work in this manner, having 1 ch-3 loop less on each row until 1 loop remains. Ch 5, turn. **Next row:** Shell over shell, ch 4, sc in ch-3 loop, ch 4, 2 dc in next shell, ch 1, sl st in sp of last shell, ch 1, 2 dc in same place as last 2 dc. Break off.

SECOND PINEAPPLE . . . With right side facing, attach thread to sp of next shell, ch 3 and complete as for First Pineapple.

THIRD AND FOURTH PINE-

APPLES . . . Work as for Second Pineapple.

Now work all around outer edges as follows: Attach thread to turning ch-5 loop preceding joining of shells at tip of pineapple, * ch 15, sc in next turning chain loop, ch 7, sc in next loop, ch 7, dc in next loop, (ch 7, tr in next loop) twice; ch 7, dc in next loop, (ch 7, sc in next loop) twice. Repeat from * around. Join.

SECOND MOTIF . . . Work as for First Motif until all 4 pineapples are completed. **Last rnd:** Attach thread to loop preceding joining of shells at tip of pineapple, ch 7, sl st in corner ch-15 loop on First Motif, ch 7, sc in next ch-5 loop on Second Motif, ch 3, sc in next ch-7 loop on First Motif, ch 3, sc in next ch-5 loop on Second Motif. Continue as for last rnd of First Motif, joining to ch-7 loops of First Motif as before until 7 ch-7 loops are joined. Ch 7, sl st in ch-15 loop of First Motif, ch 7 and complete as for First Motif (no more joinings).

Make 12 rows of 15 motifs, joining adjacent sides as Second Motif was joined to First Motif — **but do not work the last rnd on the outside edge of outer motifs.**

21

Pineapple Popcorns

MATERIALS:

J. & P. Coats or Clark's O.N.T. Pearl Cotton, Size 5: 6 balls of No. 8 Blue and 4 balls of No. 43 Dk. Yellow, or

J. & P. Coats Knit-Cro-Sheen: 2 balls of No. 70 Blue Jewel and No. 43 Dk. Yellow.

Milward's Steel Crochet Hook No. 7.

A wire napkin holder, 5 inches in diameter.

An asbestos hot plate mat, 8½ inches in diameter.

A bone ring, 3 yards of yellow ribbon, ½ inch wide.

HOT PLATE MAT . . . Starting at center with Blue, ch 4. **1st rnd:** 14 dc in 4th ch from hook. Join to top of starting chain. **2nd rnd:** Ch 6, dc in same place as sl st, * ch 3, skip 2 dc, in next dc make dc, ch 3 and dc. Repeat from * around. Join to 3rd ch of ch-6. **3rd rnd:** Drop Blue, attach Yellow, ch 3, working over unused color, make 4 dc in same sp, thread over, insert hook in same sp and draw loop through, thread over and draw through 2 loops, drop Yellow and draw loop of Blue through, thus changing color. **Always change color in this manner.** Working over unused color make 3 dc in next sp, * drop Blue, pick up Yellow, make 6 dc in next sp, drop Yellow, pick up Blue, make 3 dc in next sp. Repeat from * around, ending with 3 Blue dc. Join. **4th rnd:** Pick up Yellow, ch 4, (dc in next dc, ch 1) 4 times; dc in next dc, * drop Yellow, pick up Blue, dc in next 3 dc, drop Blue, pick up Yellow, (dc in next dc, ch 1) 5 times; dc in next dc. Repeat from * around. Join. **5th rnd:** Pick up Yellow, sl st in next sp, ch 3, 4 dc in same sp, drop loop from hook, insert hook in top of ch-3, draw dropped loop

through (pc st made), ch 2, 5 dc in next sp, drop loop from hook, insert hook in first dc, draw dropped loop through (another pc st made), (ch 2, pc st in next sp) 3 times; drop Yellow, * pick up Blue, skip next dc, 2 dc in next dc, dc in next dc, 2 dc in next dc, drop Blue, pick up Yellow, (pc st in next sp, ch 2) 4 times; pc st in next sp. Repeat from * around. Join. **6th rnd:** Pick up Yellow, sl st in next sp, ch 3, pc st in same sp, * (ch 2, pc st in next sp) 3 times; drop Yellow, pick up Blue, dc in next pc st, 2 dc in next dc, dc in each dc across to within last dc, 2 dc in next dc, dc in next pc st, drop Blue, pick up Yellow, pc st in next sp, ch 2. Repeat from * around, ending with Blue dc in first pc st. Join. **7th and 8th rnds:** Work as for 6th rnd, having 1 pc st less in each group of pc sts and 4 dc more in each dc group, until 2 pc sts remain. **9th rnd:** * Pick up Yellow, pc st in next sp, drop Yellow, pick up Blue, pc st in next dc, 2 sc in next dc, sc in each dc across to within last dc, 2 sc in last dc, sc in next pc st, drop Blue. Repeat from * around. Join. Break off Yellow. **10th rnd:** Sl st in next pc st, sl st in next sc, sc in same sc, * (ch 4, skip 3 sc, sc in next sc) 5 times; ch 4, sc in next sc. Repeat from * around. Join. **11th rnd:** Sl st to center of next loop, sc in same loop, * ch 7, sc in next loop. Repeat from * around. Join. **12th rnd:** Sl st to center of next loop, sc in same loop, * ch 8, sc in next loop. Repeat from * around. Join and break off. **13th rnd:** Attach Yellow to any loop, in each loop around make sc, half dc, 5 dc, half dc and sc. Join and break off. **14th rnd:** Attach Blue to center dc of any scallop, sc in same place, * ch 9, sc in center dc of next scallop. Repeat from * around. Join. **15th to 18th rnds incl:** Sl st to center of next loop, sc in same loop,

* ch 9, sc in next loop. Repeat from * around. Join. **19th rnd:** Sl st to center of next loop, * ch 6, sc in next loop. Repeat from * around. Join and break off. With Blue make a chain 36 inches long. Lace chain through last rnd of loops. Slip over hot plate mat, tie ends of chain securely.

POT HOLDER—Front . . . Work as for Hot Plate Mat until 11 rnds are completed. Join and break off.

BACK . . . Starting at center with Blue, ch 4. **1st rnd:** 11 dc in 4th ch from hook. Join to top of starting chain. **2nd rnd:** Ch 3, dc in same place as sl st, 2 dc in each dc around. Join. **3rd rnd:** Ch 3, dc in same place as sl st, * dc in next dc, 2 dc in next dc (1 dc increased). Repeat from * around. Join. **4th to 9th rnds incl:** Ch 3, dc in each dc around, increasing 12 dc evenly around. Join. **10th rnd:** Ch 3, dc in each dc around. Join. **11th rnd:** Ch 3, dc in each dc around, increasing 12 dc evenly around. Join and break off. **Next rnd:** Holding Front and Back pieces together and working through both pieces in order to join, attach Blue to any loop on Front and any dc on Back, sc in same place, * ch 8, skip 3 dc on Back, sc in next loop on Front and next dc on Back. Repeat from * around. Join and break off. **Following rnd:** Attach Yellow to any loop, in each loop around make sc, half dc, 5 dc, half dc and sc. Join and break off. Sc closely around bone ring. Sew bone ring in place.

NAPKIN HOLDER . . . Work as for Hot Plate Mat until 10 rnds are completed. Join and break off. Make another piece the same way. Cut yellow ribbon in half and lace pieces to napkin holder.

Pineapple Posy

Doily measures 8½ inches square

MATERIALS:

J. & P. Coats or Clark's O.N.T. Best Six Cord Mercerized Crochet, Size 30:

SMALL BALL:

J. & P. COATS—2 balls of White or Ecru, or

CLARK'S O.N.T.—2 balls of White or Ecru, or

J. & P. Coats Big Ball Best Six Cord Mercerized Crochet, Size 30: 1 ball of White or Ecru, or

Clark's Big Ball Three Cord Mercerized Crochet, Size 30, 1 ball of White or Ecru.

Milward's Steel Crochet Hook No. 10.

Starting at center, ch 6. Join with sl st to form ring. **1st rnd:** Ch 3, dc in ring, (ch 2, 2 dc in ring) 3 times; ch 2, sl st in top of ch-3. **2nd rnd:** Ch 3, dc in same place as sl st, * ch 2, 2 dc in next dc. Repeat from * around. Join. **3rd rnd:** Ch 3, dc in next dc, * ch 3, dc in next 2 dc, in next sp make dc, ch 3 and dc; dc in next 2 dc. Repeat from * around. Join. **4th rnd:** Ch 6, * 4 tr in next sp, ch 3, skip next dc, dc in next 2 dc, in next sp make dc, ch 3 and dc; dc in next 2 dc, ch 3. Repeat from * around. Join with sl st to 3rd ch of ch-6. **5th rnd:** Sl st in next 3 ch, sl st in next tr, ch 4, tr in same tr, 2 tr in each of next 3 tr; * ch 3, skip next dc, dc in next 2 dc, in next sp make dc, ch 3 and dc; dc in next 2 dc, ch 3, 2 tr in each of next 4 tr. Repeat from * around. Join. **6th rnd:** Sc in same place as sl st, * (ch 3, sc in next tr) 7 times; ch 3, skip next dc, dc in next 2 dc, in next sp make dc, ch 3 and dc; dc in next 2 dc, ch 3, sc in next tr. Repeat from * around. Join. **7th rnd:** Sl st to center of next loop, sc in same loop, * (ch 3, sc in next loop) 6 times; ch 3, skip next dc, dc in next 2 dc, in next sp make dc, ch 2, 2 dc, ch 2 and dc; dc in next 2 dc, ch 3, skip next sp, sc in next loop. Repeat from * around. Join. **8th rnd:** Sl st to center of next loop, sc in same loop, * (ch 3, sc in next loop) 5 times; ch 3, skip next dc, dc in next 2 dc, in next sp make dc, ch 3 and dc; dc in next dc, ch 2, dc in next dc, in next sp make dc, ch 3 and dc; dc in next 2 dc, ch 3, skip next sp, sc in next loop. Repeat from * around. Join. **9th rnd:** Sl st in next loop, sc in same loop,

* (ch 3, sc in next loop) 4 times; ch 3, skip next dc, dc in next 2 dc, in next sp make dc, ch 4 and dc; dc in next 2 dc, ch 3, dc in next 2 dc, in next sp make dc, ch 4 and dc; dc in next 2 dc, ch 3, skip next sp, sc in next loop. Repeat from * around. Join. **10th rnd:** Sl st in next loop, sc in same loop, * (ch 3, sc in next loop) 3 times; ch 3, skip next dc, dc in next 2 dc, in next sp make dc, ch 5 and dc; dc in next 3 dc, ch 4, dc in next 3 dc, in next sp make dc, ch 5 and dc; dc in next 2 dc, ch 3, skip next sp, sc in next loop. Repeat from * around. Join. **11th rnd:** Sl st in next loop, sc in same loop, * (ch 3, sc in next loop) twice; ch 3, skip next dc, dc in next 2 dc, in next sp make dc, ch 6 and dc; dc in next 4 dc, ch 4, dc in next 4 dc, in next sp make dc, ch 6 and dc; dc in next 2 dc, ch 3, skip next sp, sc in next loop. Repeat from * around. Join. **12th rnd:** Sl st in next loop, sc in same loop, * ch 3, sc in next loop, ch 3, skip next dc, dc in next 2 dc, dc in next sp, ch 5, 2 dc in same sp, ch 5, skip next dc, dc in next 4 dc, in next sp make dc, ch 3 and dc in next 4 dc; ch 5, 2 dc in next sp, ch 5, dc in same sp, dc in next 2 dc, ch 3, skip next sp, sc in next loop. Repeat from * around. Join. **13th rnd:** Sl st in next loop, sc in same loop, * ch 4, skip next dc, dc in next 2 dc, in next sp, ch 5, 2 dc in same sp, ch 5, 2 dc in next sp, ch 5, skip 1 dc, dc in next 4 dc, in next sp make dc, ch 3 and dc; dc in next 4 dc, (ch 5, 2 dc in next sp) twice; ch 5, dc in same sp, dc in next 2 dc, ch 4, skip next sp, sc in next loop. Repeat from * around. Join and break off. **14th rnd:** Attach thread to sp preceding last 3-dc group, ch 4, * tr in next 2 dc, skip 2 sps and next dc, tr in next 2 dc, tr in next sp, ch 5, 2 dc in same sp, (ch 5, 2 dc in next sp) twice; ch 5, skip next dc, dc in next 4 dc, dc in next 4 dc, (ch 5, 2 dc in next sp) 3 times; ch 5, tr in same sp. Repeat from * around. Join. **15th rnd:** Sc in same place as sl st, * ch 7, skip 4 tr, sc in next tr, (ch 5, 2 dc in next sp) 4 times; ch 5, skip next dc, tr in next 3 dc, ch 7, tr in next 3 dc, (ch 5, 2 dc in next sp) 4 times; ch 5, sc in next tr. Repeat from * around. Join. **16th rnd:** Sl st in next loop, ch 4, 3 tr in same loop, * ch 3, (2 dc in next sp, ch 5) 4 times; in next sp make 2 dc, ch 2 and 2 dc (shell made); ch 3, in

next sp make (2 dc, ch 2) 3 times and 2 dc; ch 3, in next sp make 2 dc, ch 2 and 2 dc; (ch 5, 2 dc in next sp) 4 times; ch 3, 4 tr in next loop. Repeat from * around. Join. **17th rnd:** Ch 4, tr in same place as sl st, 2 tr in each of next 3 tr, * ch 3, skip next sp, (2 dc in next sp, ch 5) 3 times; skip next sp, in sp of next shell make 2 dc, ch 2 and 2 dc (shell made over shell); ch 3, skip next sp, 8 tr in next sp, shell in next sp, 8 tr in next sp, ch 3, skip next sp, shell over next shell, ch 5, skip next sp, (2 dc in next sp, ch 5) 2 times; 2 dc in next sp, ch 3, 2 tr in each of next 4 tr. Repeat from * around. Join. **18th rnd:** Sc in same place as sl st, * (ch 3, sc in next tr) 7 times; ch 3, dc in next 2 dc, dc in next sp, ch 5, 2 dc in next sp, ch 5, shell over next shell, (ch 3, sc in next tr) 8 times; ch 1, shell over shell, ch 1, sc in next tr, (ch 3, sc in next tr) 7 times; ch 3, shell over shell, ch 5, skip next sp, 2 dc in next sp, ch 5, dc in next sp, dc in next 2 dc, ch 3, sc in next tr. Repeat from * around. Join. **19th rnd:** Sl st in next loop, sc in same loop, * (ch 3, sc in next loop) 6 times; ch 3, skip next dc, dc in next 2 dc, in next sp make dc, ch 4 and dc; dc in next dc, ch 1, dc in next dc, dc in next sp, ch 4, shell over shell, ch 3, skip next sp, sc in next loop, (ch 3, sc in next loop) 6 times; ch 1, shell over shell, ch 1, (sc in next loop, ch 3) 7 times; shell over shell, ch 4, dc in next sp, dc in next dc, ch 1, dc in next dc, in next sp make dc, ch 4 and dc; dc in next 2 dc, ch 3, skip next sp, sc in next loop. Repeat from * around. Join. **20th rnd:** Sl st in next loop, sc in same loop, * (ch 3, sc in next loop) 5 times; ch 3, skip next dc, dc in next 2 dc, in next sp make dc, ch 3 and dc; dc in next 2 dc, ch 2, dc in next 2 dc, dc in next sp, ch 3, shell over shell, ch 3, skip next sp, sc in next loop, (ch 3, sc in next loop) 5 times; ch 1, in sp of next shell make (2 dc, ch 2) twice and 2 dc; ch 1, sc in next loop, (ch 3, sc in next loop) 5 times; ch 3, shell over shell, ch 3, dc in next sp, dc in next 2 dc, ch 2, dc in next 2 dc, in next sp make dc, ch 3 and dc; dc in next 2 dc, ch 3, skip next sp, sc in next loop. Repeat from * around. Join.

21st rnd: Sl st in next loop, sc in same loop, * (ch 3, sc in next loop) 4 times; ch 3, skip next dc, dc in next 2 dc, in next sp make dc, ch 2 and dc;

dc in next 3 dc, ch 3, dc in next 3 dc, dc in next sp, ch 2, shell over shell, ch 3, skip next sp, (sc in next loop, ch 3) 5 times; shell in next ch-2 sp, ch 1, shell in next sp, ch 3, skip next sp, (sc in next loop, ch 3) 5 times; shell over shell, ch 2, dc in next sp, dc in next 3 dc, ch 3, dc in next 3 dc, in next sp make dc, ch 2 and dc; dc in next 2 dc, ch 3, skip next sp, sc in next loop. Repeat. from * around. Join. **22nd rnd:** Sl st in next loop, sc in same loop, * (ch 3, sc in next loop) 3 times; ch 3, skip next dc, dc in next 2 dc, in next sp make dc, ch 1 and dc; dc in next 4 dc, ch 3, dc in next 4 dc, dc in next sp, ch 1, shell over shell, ch 3, skip next sp, (sc in next loop, ch 3) 4 times; (shell over shell, ch 3) twice; skip next sp, (sc in next loop, ch 3) 4 times; shell over shell, ch 1, dc in next sp, dc in next 4 dc, ch 3, dc in next 4 dc, in next sp make dc, ch 1 and dc; dc in next 2 dc, ch 3, skip next sp, sc in next loop. Repeat from * around. Join. **23rd rnd:** Sl st in next loop, sc in same loop, * (ch 3, sc in next loop) twice; ch 3, skip next dc, dc in next 2 dc, in next sp, dc in next 2 dc, skip next dc, dc in next 4 dc, in next sp make dc, ch 3 and dc; dc in next 4 dc, ch 2, shell over shell, ch 3, skip next sp, (sc in next loop, ch 3) 3 times; shell over

shell, ch 3, 3 tr in center ch of next sp, ch 3, shell over shell, ch 3, skip next sp, (sc in next loop, ch 3) 3 times; shell over shell, ch 2, skip next dc, dc in next 4 dc, in next sp make dc, ch 3 and dc; dc in next 4 dc, ch 2, dc in next sp, dc in next 2 dc, ch 3, skip next sp, sc in next loop. Repeat from * around. Join.

24th rnd: Sl st in next loop, sc in same loop, * ch 3, sc in next loop, ch 3, skip next dc, dc in next 2 dc, dc in next sp, ch 3, skip next dc, dc in next 4 dc, in next sp make dc, ch 2 and dc; dc in next 4 dc, ch 3, shell over shell, ch 3, skip next sp, (sc in next loop, ch 3) twice; shell over shell, ch 5, 2 tr in each of next 3 tr, ch 5, shell over shell, ch 3, skip next sp, (sc in next loop, ch 3) twice; shell over shell, ch 3, skip next dc, dc in next 4 dc, in next sp make dc, ch 2 and dc; dc in next 4 dc, ch 3, dc in next sp, dc in next 2 dc, ch 3, skip next sp, sc in next loop. Repeat from * around. Join. **25th rnd:** Sl st in next loop, sc in same loop, * ch 4, skip next dc, dc in next 2 dc, dc in next sp, ch 4, skip next dc, dc in next 4 dc, ch 1, dc in next 4 dc, ch 4, shell over shell, ch 4, skip next sp, sc in next loop, ch 4, shell over shell, ch 7, (tr in next tr, ch 3) 5 times; tr in next tr, ch 7, shell over shell, ch 4,

skip next sp, sc in next loop, ch 4, shell over shell, ch 4, skip next dc, dc in next 4 dc, ch 1, dc in next 4 dc, ch 4, dc in next sp, dc in next 2 dc, ch 4, skip next sp, sc in next loop. Repeat from * around. Join. **26th rnd:** Sl st in next 4 ch, sl st in next 2 dc, ch 3, dc in next dc, * dc in next sp, ch 8, skip next dc, dc in next 3 dc, dc in next sp, dc in next 3 dc, ch 8, shell over each of next 2 shells, ch 8, skip next sp, sc in next sp, (ch 5, sc in next sp) 4 times; ch 8, shell over each of next 2 shells, ch 8, skip next dc, dc in next 3 dc, dc in next sp, dc in next 3 dc, ch 8, dc in next sp, dc in next 2 dc, skip 2 dc, dc in next 2 dc. Repeat from * around. Join. **27th rnd:** Sc in same place as sl st, sc in next 2 dc, * in next sp make 5 sc, ch 3 and 5 sc; sc in next 7 dc, in next sp make 5 sc, ch 3 and 5 sc; sc in next 2 dc, sc in next sp, ch 3, sc in next sp, sc in next 2 dc, in next sp make 5 sc, ch 3 and 5 sc; in each of next 4 sps make 3 sc, ch 3 and 3 sc; in next sp make 5 sc, ch 3 and 5 sc; sc in next 2 dc, sc in next sp, ch 3, sc in next sp, sc in next 2 dc, in next sp make 5 sc, ch 3 and 5 sc; sc in next 7 dc, in next sp make 5 sc, ch 3 and 5 sc; sc in next 6 dc. Repeat from * around. Join and break off. Starch lightly and press.

TEA APRON

GUEST TOWEL

FRINGED GUEST TOWEL

BATH TOWEL SET

PILLOW CASE

26

Pineapple Trousseau

Bath Towel Set

MATERIALS:

CLARK'S BIG BALL MERCERIZED CROCHET, Art. B.34, Size 30: 1 ball of No. 123-A Flamingo; or

J. & P. COATS BEST SIX CORD MERCERIZED CROCHET, Art. A.104, Size 30: 1 ball of No. 123-A Flamingo; or

CLARK'S O.N.T. BEST SIX CORD MERCERIZED CROCHET, Art. B.4, Size 30: 3 balls of any color.

Milwards Steel Crochet Hook No. 10.

A chartreuse bath towel, hand towel and washcloth.

BATH TOWEL . . . Starting at long side, make a chain slightly longer than edge of towel. **1st row:** Sc in 2nd ch from hook, * ch 5, skip 2 ch, sc in next 9 ch. Repeat from * across until row is long enough to reach across towel, ending with ch 5, skip 2 ch, sc in next ch. Cut off remaining chain. Turn. **2nd row:** Sl st in first loop, ch 3, 8 dc in same loop, * ch 1, skip 4 sc, dc in next sc, ch 1, 9 dc in next loop. Repeat from * across. Ch 1, turn. **3rd row:** Sc in first dc, * (ch 1, sc in next dc) 8 times; ch 3, skip next dc, sc in next dc. Repeat from * across, ending with sc in top of turning chain. Ch 1, turn. **4th row:** Sc in first sp, * (ch 1, sc in next sp) 7 times; ch 3, skip next sp, sc in next sp. Repeat from * across. Ch 1, turn. **5th and 6th rows:** Work as for 4th row, having 1 sp less on each pineapple on each row and making ch-4 between pineapples on 5th row and ch-5 on 6th row. **7th row:** Sc in first sp, * (ch 1, sc in next sp) 4 times; (ch 3, sc in next sp) twice. Repeat from * across. Ch 1, turn. **8th row:** Sc in first sp, * (ch 1, sc in next sp) 3 times; ch 3, sc in next sp, sc in next sc, sc in next sp, ch 3, sc in next sp. Repeat from * across. Ch 1, turn. **9th row:** Sc in first sp, * (ch 1, sc in next sp) twice; ch 3, sc in next sp, sc in next 3 sc, sc in next sp, ch 3, sc in next sp. Repeat from * across. Ch 1, turn. **10th row:** Sc in first sp, * ch 1, (sc in next sp, ch 3) twice; skip next sc, sc in next 3 sc, (ch 3, sc in next sp) twice. Repeat from * across. Ch 4, turn. **11th row:** Holding back on hook the last loop of each tr make tr in next 2 sps, thread over and draw through all loops on hook (joint-tr made), * ch 9, make a joint-tr by making tr in next sp, in center sc of next 3-sc group and in next sp; ch 9, make a joint-tr over next 3 sps. Repeat from * across, ending with joint-tr over last 2 sps and last sc. Break off.

Starch edging lightly. Sew to towel.

HAND TOWEL . . . Work exactly as for Bath Towel.

WASHCLOTH . . . 1st rnd: Attach thread to edge of washcloth and sc closely around. Join. **2nd rnd:** Sc in same place as sl st, * ch 3, skip 2 sc, sc in next sc. Repeat from * around, having an even number of loops. **3rd rnd:** Sl st in next loop, ch 4, make a joint-tr over next 2 loops, * ch 9, make a joint-tr by making tr in same loop as last tr and in next 2 loops. Repeat from * around. Join and break off.

Pillow Case

MATERIALS:

CLARK'S BIG BALL MERCERIZED CROCHET, Art. B.34, Size 30: 3 balls of No. 65 Beauty Pink; or

J. & P. COATS BEST SIX CORD MERCERIZED CROCHET, Art. A.104, Size 30: 3 balls of No. 4-A Mid Pink; or

CLARK'S O.N.T. BEST SIX CORD MERCERIZED CROCHET, Art. B.4, Size 30: 10 balls of No. 4-A Mid Pink.

Milwards Steel Crochet Hook No. 10.

A matching pillow case.

Starting at narrow end, ch 8. **1st row:** In 8th ch from hook make 2 dc, ch 2 and 2 dc (shell made). Ch 7, turn. **2nd row:** In sp of shell make 2 dc, ch 2 and 2 dc (shell made over shell). Ch 7, turn. Repeat 2nd row until piece is slightly longer than edge of pillow case, having a number of loops on each side divisible by 3. Break off. Sew narrow ends together.

HEADING . . . Attach thread to first loop made, sc in same loop, * ch 6, sc in next loop. Repeat from * around. Join with sl st to first sc. Break off.

EDGING . . . 1st rnd: Attach thread to first loop on opposite side of Heading, sc in same loop, * ch 7, sc in next loop, ch 3, 9 tr in next loop, ch 3, sc in next loop. Repeat from * around. Join. **2nd rnd:** Sl st to center of first loop, sc in same loop, * ch 7, (tr in next tr, ch 1) 8 times; tr in next tr, ch 7, skip next sp, sc in next loop. Repeat from * around. Join. **3rd rnd:** Sl st to center of next loop, sc in same loop, * ch 7, (sc in next ch-1 sp, ch 2) 7 times; sc in next ch-1 sp, (ch 7, sc in next loop) twice. Repeat from * around. Join. **4th rnd:** Sl st to center of next loop, sc in same loop, * ch 7, (5 dc in next ch-2 loop, drop loop from hook, insert hook in first dc, draw dropped loop through—pc st made—ch 2) 6 times; pc st in next ch-2 loop, (ch 7, sc in next loop) 3 times. Repeat from * around. Join. **5th rnd:** Sl st to center of next loop, sc in same loop, * ch 7, (sc in next ch-2 sp, ch 2) 5 times; sc in next ch-2 sp, (ch 7, sc in next loop) 4 times. Repeat from * around. Join. **6th rnd:** Sl st to center of next loop, * ch 7, (pc st in next ch-2 loop, ch 2) 4 times; pc st in next ch-2 loop, (ch 7, sc in next loop) 5 times. Repeat from * around. Join. Continue working in this manner, having 1 ch-2 loop less on each pineapple on every other rnd and 1 more ch-7 loop between pineapples on each rnd until 1 pc st remains. **Next rnd:** Sl st to center of next loop, sc in same loop, * ch 7, sc in next loop. Repeat from * around. Break off.

Sew edging neatly in place. Starch lightly and press.

Guest Towel

MATERIALS:

CLARK'S BIG BALL MERCERIZED CROCHET, Art. B.34, Size 30: 1 ball of No. 49 Chartreuse Green; or

J. & P. COATS BEST SIX CORD MERCERIZED CROCHET, Art. A.104, Size 30: 1 ball of No. 49 Chartreuse Green; or

CLARK'S O.N.T. BEST SIX CORD MERCERIZED CROCHET, Art. B.4, Size 30: 2 balls of any color.

Milwards Steel Crochet Hook No. 10.

A yellow guest towel.

Starting at narrow end, ch 10. **1st row:** In 10th ch from hook make 2 dc, ch 2 and 2 dc (shell made). Ch 7, turn. **2nd row:** In sp of shell make 2 dc, ch 2 and 2 dc (shell made over shell); 9 tr in ch-10 loop. Ch 7, turn. **3rd row:** (Tr in next tr, ch 1) 9 times; shell over shell. Ch 7, turn. **4th row:** Shell over shell, ch 2, skip next sp, (sc in next sp, ch 2) 7 times; sc in next sp. Ch 7, turn. **5th row:** 5 dc in first loop, drop loop from hook, insert hook in first dc of group, draw dropped loop through (pc st made); (ch 2, pc st in next loop) 6 times; ch 3, shell over shell. Ch 7, turn. **6th row:** Shell over shell, ch 5, skip next sp, sc in next sp, (ch 2, sc in next sp) 5 times. Ch 7, turn. **7th row:** Pc st in first loop, (ch 2, pc st in next loop) 4 times; ch 5, sc in next loop, ch 5, shell over shell. Ch 7, turn. **8th row:** Shell over shell, ch 5, sc in next loop, sc in next sc, sc in next loop, ch 5, sc in next sp, (ch 2, sc in next sp) 3 times. Ch 7, turn. **9th row:** Pc st in first loop, (ch 2, pc st in next loop) twice; ch 5, sc in next loop, sc in next 3 sc, sc in next loop, ch 5, shell over shell. Ch 7, turn. **10th row:** Shell over shell, ch 5, sc in next loop, sc in next 5 sc, sc in next loop, ch 5, sc in next sp, ch 2, sc in next sp. Ch 7, turn. **11th row:** Pc st in first loop, ch 5, * sc in next loop, ch 9, sc in next loop, ch 5, shell over shell. Ch 7, turn. **12th row:** Shell over shell, 9 tr in next loop, sc in next loop. Ch 7, turn. Repeat 3rd to 12th rows incl until piece is length desired, ending with 10th row. Ch 7, turn. **Next row:** Pc st in first loop, ch 5, sc in next loop, ch 9, sc in next loop. Break off.

HEADING . . . Attach thread to first ch-7 loop on opposite side, sc in same loop, * ch 6, sc in next loop. Repeat from * across. Break off.

Starch edging lightly and press. Sew neatly to edge of towel.

Fringed Guest Towel

MATERIALS:

CLARK'S BIG BALL MERCERIZED CROCHET, Art. B.34, Size 30: 1 ball of White; or

J. & P. COATS BEST SIX CORD MERCERIZED CROCHET, Art. A.104, Size 30: 1 ball of White; or

CLARK'S O.N.T. BEST SIX CORD MERCERIZED CROCHET, Art. B.4, Size 30: 2 balls of White.

Milwards Steel Crochet Hook No. 10.

A blue guest towel.

Starting at narrow end, ch 20. **1st row:** In 8th ch from hook make 2 dc, ch 2 and 2 dc (shell made); ch 7, skip next 4 ch, sc in next ch, ch 3, skip next ch, sc in next ch, ch 7, skip next 4 ch, in next ch make 2 dc, ch 2 and 2 dc (another shell made). Ch 7, turn. **2nd row:** Shell in sp of shell (shell made over shell), ch 4, sc in next loop, ch 5, skip next ch-3 loop, sc in next loop, ch 4, shell over next shell. Ch 7, turn. **3rd row:** Shell over shell, ch 1, skip next loop, 9 tr in next loop, ch 1, shell over next shell. Ch 7, turn. **4th row:** Shell over shell, ch 3, sc in next tr, (ch 3, skip next tr, sc in next tr) 4 times; ch 3, shell over shell. Ch 7, turn. **5th row:** Shell over shell, ch 4, skip next sp, (sc in next loop, ch 3) 3 times; sc in next loop, ch 4, shell over shell. Ch 7, turn. **6th row:** Shell over shell, ch 5, skip next sp, (sc in next loop, ch 3) twice; sc in next loop, ch 5, shell over shell. Ch 7, turn. **7th row:** Shell over shell, ch 7, skip next sp, sc in next loop, ch 3, sc in next loop, ch 7, shell over shell. Ch 7, turn. Repeat 2nd to 7th rows incl until piece is length desired, ending with 7th row. **Next row:** Shell over shell, ch 5, skip next sp, tr in next loop, ch 5, shell over shell. Break off.

HEADING . . . Attach thread to first ch-7 loop on long side, sc in same loop, * ch 5, sc in next loop. Repeat from * across. Break off.

Starch edging lightly and press. Sew to towel.

FRINGE . . . Cut 8 strands of thread, each 5 inches long. Double strands to form a loop, insert hook in first ch-7 loop on opposite side, draw loop through. Draw loose ends through loop and pull up tightly to form a knot. Make a fringe in each turning chain loop across. Trim ends evenly.

Tea Apron

MATERIALS:

CLARK'S BIG BALL MERCERIZED CROCHET, Art. B.34, Size 30: 2 balls of No. 123-A Flamingo; or

J. & P. COATS BEST SIX CORD MERCERIZED CROCHET, Art. A.104, Size 30: 2 balls of No. 123-A Flamingo; or

CLARK'S O.N.T. BEST SIX CORD MERCERIZED CROCHET, Art. B.4, Size 30: 4 balls of any color.

Milwards Steel Crochet Hook No. 10.

A dark green organdy tea apron.

EDGING . . . Starting at long side, make a chain slightly longer than apron. **1st row:** 2 dc in 4th ch from hook, skip 5 ch, * 9 tr in next ch, skip 5 ch, 3 dc in next ch, ch 4, skip 5 ch, 3 dc in next ch. Repeat from * across, until row is long enough to reach around apron, ending with 9 tr, skip 3 ch, 3 dc in next ch. Cut off remaining chain. Ch 3, turn. **2nd row:** Skip first dc, dc in next 2 dc, * (ch 1, tr in next tr) 9 times; ch 1, dc in next 3 dc, ch 4, dc in next 3 dc. Repeat from * across, ending with dc in top of turning chain. Ch 3, turn. **3rd row:** Skip first dc, dc in next 2 dc, * ch 2, skip next sp, (sc in next sp, ch 3) 7 times; sc in next sp, ch 2, dc in next 3 dc, ch 3, dc in next 3 dc. Repeat from * across, ending with dc in top of turning chain. Ch 3, turn. **4th row:** Skip first dc, dc in next 2 dc, * ch 3, skip next sp, (sc in next loop, ch 3) 7 times; dc in next 3 dc, ch 2, dc in next 3 dc. Repeat from * across, ending with dc in top of turning chain. Ch 3, turn. **5th row:** Skip first dc, dc in next 2 dc, * ch 4, skip next sp, (sc in next loop, ch 3) 5 times; sc in next loop, ch 4, dc in next 3 dc, ch 3, dc in next 3 dc. Repeat from * across. Ch 3, turn. **6th row:** Skip first dc, dc in next 2 dc, * ch 4, skip next sp, (sc in next loop, ch 3) 4 times; sc in next loop, ch 4, dc in next 3 dc, ch 4, dc in next 3 dc. Repeat from * across, ending with dc in top of turning chain. Ch 3, turn. **7th row:** Skip first dc, dc in next 2 dc, * ch 4, skip next sp, (sc in next loop, ch 3) 3 times; sc in next loop, ch 4, dc in next 3 dc, (ch 5, sc in 3rd ch from hook—picot made) twice; ch 2, sc in next sp (picot loop made), make another picot loop, dc in next 3 dc. Repeat from * across, ending with dc in top of turning chain. Ch 3, turn.
8th row: Skip first dc, dc in next 2 dc, * ch 4, skip 1 sp, (sc in next loop, ch 3) twice; sc in next loop, ch 4, dc in next 3 dc, (make a picot loop, sc in next loop between picots) twice; make a picot loop, dc in next 3 dc. Repeat from * across, ending with dc in top of turning chain. Ch 3, turn. **9th row:** Skip first dc, dc in next 2 dc, * ch 4, skip next sp, sc in next loop, ch 3, sc in next loop, ch 4, dc in next 3 dc, (make a picot loop, sc in next loop between picots) 3 times; make a picot loop, dc in next 3 dc. Repeat from * across, ending with dc in top of turning chain. Ch 3, turn. **10th row:** Skip first dc, dc in next 2 dc, * ch 4, skip next sp, sc in next loop, ch 4, dc in next 3 dc, (make a picot loop, sc in next loop between picots) 4 times; make a picot loop, dc in next 3 dc. Repeat from * across, ending with dc in top of turning chain. Ch 3, turn. **11th row:** Skip first dc, holding back on hook the last loop of each dc make dc in next 2 dc, thread over and draw through all loops on hook (cluster made), * make a cluster over next 3 dc, (make a picot loop, sc in next loop between picots) 5 times; make a picot loop, cluster over next 3 dc. Repeat from * across, ending with cluster, having last dc in top of turning chain. Break off.

Starch edging lightly and press. Sew to Apron.

Pineapple Handkerchief Edging

9187 Materials: J. & P. Coats Tatting-Crochet, *Size 70, 4 balls of White . . . Steel Crochet Hook No. 13 . . . A hemstitched handkerchief, 11½ inches square.*

1st rnd: Attach thread to one corner, * 3 sc in corner, then make 157 sc across to next corner. Repeat from * around. Join with sl st (640 sc in all). **2nd rnd:** Sl st in next 3 sc, ch 6, ** (skip 1 sc, dc in next sc, ch 3) twice; * skip 2 sc, dc in next sc, ch 3. Repeat from * to within 3 sc from corner 3-sc group, (ch 3, skip 1 sc, dc in next sc) twice; (ch 3, dc in next sc) twice; ch 3. Repeat from ** around. Join last ch-3 to 3rd ch of ch-6 (56 sps on each side, including 1 sp of each corner). **3rd rnd:** Sl st in next sp, sc in same sp, (ch 5, sc in next sp) 4 times; * ch 10, skip next sp, sc in next sp, (ch 5, sc in next sp) 5 times. Repeat from * around. Join. **4th rnd:** Sl st to center of next loop, (ch 5, sc in next loop) 3 times; * ch 3, 10 tr in ch-10 loop, ch 3, sc in next loop, (ch 5, sc in next loop) 4 times. Repeat from * around. Join. **5th rnd:** Sl st to center of loop, (ch 5, sc in next loop) twice; * ch 3, (tr in next tr, ch 1) 9 times; tr in next tr, ch 3, sc in next ch-5 loop, (ch 5, sc in next loop) 3 times. Repeat from * around. Join. **6th rnd:** Sl st to center of loop, ch 5, sc in next loop, * ch 3, 3 dc in ch-3 sp, (ch 3, sc in next ch-1 sp) 9 times; ch 3, 3 dc in next sp, ch 3, sc in next loop, (ch 5, sc in next ch-5 loop) twice. Repeat from * around. Join. **7th rnd:** Sl st to center of loop, * ch 5, skip 3 dc, 3 dc in next loop, (ch 3, sc in next loop) 8 times; ch 3, 3 dc in next loop, (ch 5, sc in next ch-5 loop) twice. Repeat from * around, ending with ch 2, dc at base of starting chain. **8th rnd:** * Ch 7, skip 3 dc, 3 dc in ch-3 loop, (ch 3, sc in next loop) 7 times; ch 3, 3 dc in ch-3 loop, ch 7, skip 3 dc and ch 5, sc in next loop. Repeat from * around, ending with ch 7, sl st in dc. Break off.

Now work pineapples individually as follows: **1st row:** Attach thread to first ch-3 loop following the 3-dc group, ch 5, 3 dc in same loop, (ch 3, sc in next loop) 6 times; ch 3, 3 dc in next ch-3 loop. Ch 5, turn. **2nd row:** 3 dc in next ch-3 loop, (ch 3, sc in next loop) 5 times; ch 3, 3 dc in next ch-3 loop. Ch 5, turn. **3rd, 4th and 5th rows:** Continue in this manner, having one ch-3 loop less on each row (one ch-3 loop remains on 5th row). **6th row:** 3 dc in next ch-3 loop, ch 3, sc in next loop, ch 3, 3 dc in next ch-3 loop. Ch 5, turn. **7th row:** (3 dc in next ch-3 loop) twice. Ch 5, turn, sl st between the two 3-dc groups. Break off. Work all pineapples in same manner. Attach thread to first ch-5 loop preceding the first 3-dc group on first pineapple, * ch 10, sc in next ch-5 loop. Repeat from * across, ending with sc in last free ch-5 loop of same pineapple, ch 7, (sc in next ch-7 loop) twice; ch 7, sc in next free ch-5 loop on next pineapple, ch 10, sc in next ch-5 loop and continue thus around. Break off.

29

Pineapple Flower Girl

A new version of the ever favorite pineapple design in a charming party dress to make a toddler look like a rose bud.

Sizes 2 and 4

MATERIALS: J. & P. COATS or CLARK'S O.N.T. BEST SIX CORD MERCERIZED CROCHET, *Size 30:*

Use one of the following	Size 2	Size 4
SMALL BALL: J. & P. COATS	7 balls of White or Ecru, or 10 balls of any color.	9 balls of White or Ecru, or 11 balls of any color.
SMALL BALL: CLARK'S O.N.T.	10 balls of White or Ecru, or 11 balls of any color.	11 balls of White or Ecru, or 13 balls of any color.
BIG BALL: J. & P. COATS	4 balls of White, Ecru or Cream.	5 balls of White, Ecru or Cream.

Steel Crochet Hook No. 10 or 11.
5 small pearl buttons.   2½ yards of narrow velvet ribbon.

Sizes	2	4
FINISHED MEASUREMENTS:		
Length from shoulder to bottom of Skirt	16"	18"
Width at hem	48"	54"

GAUGE: (Yoke) 2 shells and 2 sps measure 1 inch; 5 rows of shells measure 1 inch.

Sizes	2	4

BODICE—Front . . . Make a chain about 20 inches long (14 ch sts to an inch). **1st row:** In 5th ch from hook make 2 dc, ch 2 and 2 dc (shell is made), * ch 2, skip 5 ch, make a shell in next ch. Repeat from * across until there are in all **22** (**24**) shells. Cut off remaining chain. Ch 3, turn.

2nd row: * Shell in sp of shell (shell over shell is made), ch 2. Repeat from * across. Ch 3, turn. Repeat 2nd row until **7** (**10**) rows in all are made, omitting turning ch on last row.

To Shape Armholes: Sl st in next dc, in the following ch, and in sp (shell is decreased), ch 5, * shell over next shell, ch 2. Repeat from * across, ending with shell over next to last shell (another shell is decreased). Turn. Repeat this last row once more. Work straight in pattern until **21** (**24**) rows in all are made. **Next row:** Work in pattern across **5** (**6**) shells. Ch 3, turn.

Work in pattern over this section only until **28** (**31**) rows in all are made. Work 2 more rows in shell pattern over this section, shaping shoulders by decreasing 2 shells at both ends of armhole edges on each row— *to dec 2 shells at beginning of row, sl st across 1 shell and up to center of next shell, ch 3, shell over next shell:—to dec 2 shells at end of row, work to within last 2 shells.* Fasten off. Skip 8 shells for neck and work other shoulder to correspond.

RIGHT BACK . . . Make a chain about 10 inches long. **1st row:** Work as for 1st row of Front until there are **11** (**12**) shells. Cut off remaining chain. Ch 3, turn. Work straight in shell pattern, keeping center back edge straight and shaping armhole and shoulder as for Front.

LEFT BACK . . . Work to correspond with Right Back. Sew shoulders and underarm seams (edge to edge).

BEADING . . . **1st row:** Attach thread in sp of 1st shell of Right Back at foundation chain, sc in same place, make **243 sc** (**261 sc**) in all along bottom of all 3 sections of Bodice, making ch 5 between sections. Ch 5, turn. **2nd row:** Ch 5, in 1st sc make d tr, ch 4 and 2 d tr; * skip 8 sts, in next st make 2 d tr, ch 4 and 2 d tr. Repeat from * across. There are in all **29** (**31**) ch-4 sps. Ch 3, turn.

SKIRT . . . **1st row:** * Shell in next ch-4 sp, ch 5. Repeat from * across. There are in all **29** (**31**) shells. Ch 3, turn. **2nd row:** Make shell over shell, having ch 6 between shells. Ch 3, turn.

Hereafter "shell over shell" will be referred to as "s.o.s.".

3rd row: * S.o.s., ch 7, in sp of next shell make 2 dc, ch 5 and 2 dc; ch 7. Repeat from * across. Fasten off. Place the 2 end shells over each other and sew in place. Work over them as if they were 1 shell.

Hereafter work is done in rnds: **1st rnd:** Attach thread in ch-5 sp of next shell, ch 4, 12 tr in same sp, * ch 5, s.o.s., ch 5, 13 tr in ch-5 sp of next shell. Repeat from * around, ending with ch 5. Join to 4th st of ch-4. **2nd rnd:** Ch 5 (to count as tr and ch 1), tr in next tr; (ch 1, tr in next tr) 11 times; * ch 4, s.o.s., ch 4, tr in next tr; (ch 1, tr in next tr) 12 times. Repeat from * around; join to 4th st of ch-5 first made. **3rd rnd:** Sl st in 1st ch-1 sp, sc in same sp; *(ch 3, sc in next ch-1 sp) 11 times; ch 4, s.o.s., ch 4, sc in next ch-1 sp. Repeat from * around, ending with ch 4, sc in 1st ch-3 loop. **4th rnd:** * (Ch 3, sc in next loop) 10 times; ch 4, s.o.s., ch 4, sc in next ch-3 loop. Repeat from * around, ending as for previous rnd. **5th rnd:** * (Ch 3, sc in next loop) 9 times; ch 4, in ch-2 sp of next shell make 2 dc, ch 2, 2 dc, ch 2 and 2 dc; ch 4, sc in next loop. Repeat from * around, ending as before. **6th rnd:** * (Ch 3, sc in next loop) 8 times; ch 4, in next ch-2 sp make a shell; ch 2, shell in next ch-2 sp, ch 4, sc in next loop. Repeat from * around, ending as before. **7th rnd:** * (Ch 3, sc in next loop) 7 times; ch 4, s.o.s.,

Continued on page 32.

Flower Girl

Continued from page 31.

ch 1, shell in next ch-2 sp, ch 1, s.o.s., ch 4, sc in next loop. Repeat from * around, ending as before. **8th rnd:** * (Ch 3, sc in next loop) 6 times; ch 4, s.o.s., (ch 2, s.o.s.) twice; ch 4, sc in next loop. Repeat from * around, ending as before. **9th rnd:** * (Ch 3, sc in next loop) 5 times; ch 4, s.o.s., (ch 4, s.o.s.) twice; ch 4, sc in next loop. Repeat from * around. **10th rnd:** * (Ch 3, sc in next loop) 4 times; ch 4, s.o.s., ch 5; in next shell make 2 dc, ch 5 and 2 dc; ch 5, s.o.s., ch 4, sc in next loop. Repeat from * around. **11th rnd:** * (Ch 3, sc in next loop) 3 times; ch 4, s.o.s., ch 4, 14 tr in next shell, ch 4, s.o.s., ch 4, sc in next loop. Repeat from * around.

12th rnd: * (Ch 3, sc in next loop) twice; ch 4, s.o.s., ch 4, tr in next tr; (ch 1, tr in next tr) 13 times; ch 4, s.o.s., ch 4, sc in next loop. Repeat from * around. **13th rnd:** * Ch 3, sc in next loop, ch 4, s.o.s., ch 4, sc in next ch-1 sp, (ch 3, sc in next ch-1 sp) 12 times; ch 4, s.o.s., ch 4, sc in next loop. Repeat from * around. **14th rnd:** * Ch 4, s.o.s., ch 4, sc in next loop, (ch 3, sc in next loop) 11 times; ch 4, s.o.s., ch 4, sc in next loop. Repeat from * around, ending with ch 4, sl st in 1st sc of previous rnd. **15th rnd:** Sl st to sp of shell, ch 3, dc in same place, ch 2, 2 dc in same place, * ch 4, sc in next loop, (ch 3, sc in next loop) 10 times; ch 4, s.o.s., ch 3, s.o.s. Repeat from * around, ending with ch 3, join to top of ch-3 first made. **16th rnd:** Sl st to sp of shell, ch 3, dc in same place, ch 2, 2 dc in same place. * Ch 4, sc in next loop, (ch 3, sc in next loop) 9 times; ch 4, s.o.s., ch 1, shell in next ch-3 sp, ch 1, s.o.s. Repeat from * around. Join. **17th rnd:** Make a shell,

then * ch 4, sc in next loop, (ch 3, sc in next loop) 8 times; ch 4, s.o.s., (ch 3, s.o.s.) twice. Repeat from * around. Join. **18th rnd:** Shell, * ch 4, sc in next loop, (ch 3, sc in next loop) 7 times; (ch 4, s.o.s.) 3 times. Repeat from * around. Join. **19th rnd:** Shell, * ch 4, sc in next loop, (ch 3, sc in next loop) 6 times; ch 4, s.o.s., ch 5, in next shell make 2 dc, ch 6 and 2 dc; ch 5, s.o.s. Repeat from * around. **20th rnd:** Shell, * ch 4, sc in next loop, (ch 3, sc in next loop) 5 times; ch 4, s.o.s., ch 4, in ch-6 loop make 15 tr; ch 4, s.o.s. Repeat from * around (3rd pineapple rnd started). Continue in established pattern around until only 1 loop remains on pineapples of 2nd pineapple rnd.

Next rnd: S.o.s., * ch 4, sc in next loop, ch 4, s.o.s., ch 4, sc in next loop, (ch 3, sc in next loop) 10 times; ch 4, s.o.s. Repeat from * around. Join. This completes 2nd pineapple rnd. Continue working in this manner until 5 pineapple rnds have been completed, having 15 tr for pineapples of 4th and 5th pineapple rnds. Join. **Next rnd:** * S.o.s., ch 3, s.o.s., ch 4, sc in next loop, (ch 3, sc in next loop) 10 times. Repeat from * around. Join. Now work pineapples individually as follows: **1st row:** S.o.s., ch 4, sc in next loop, (ch 3, sc in next loop) 9 times; ch 4, s.o.s. Ch 5, turn. Continue in this manner, having one ch-3 loop less on each row until 1 loop remains at top of pineapple. Ch 5, turn. **Next row:** Make s.o.s., ch 4, sc in loop, ch 4, s.o.s. Ch 5, turn, make s.o.s. twice. Fasten off. Attach thread to 1st shell of next pineapple and complete the point in same manner. Continue thus until all points have been worked.

Work 2 rnds all around outer edges as follows: **1st rnd:** Attach thread in ch-3 sp between shells (at base of points), sc in same place, * shell over each turning ch along both sides of point and in each of the 2 shells at tip of point, having ch-2 between shells;

sc in next ch-3 between shells (at base of points). Repeat from * around. Join. **2nd rnd:** Sl st to center of next shell, ch 5, * sc in next ch-2 sp, ch 2, in sp of next shell make dc, p and dc—*to make a p, ch 4 and sc in 4th ch from hook;* ch 2. Repeat from * across point, ending with ch 2, dc in sp of last shell on this point, dc in sp of 1st shell on next point, ch 2, sc in next ch-2 sp, ch 2, in sp of next shell make dc, p and dc and continue thus around. Join and fasten off.

SLEEVES . . . 1st rnd: Attach thread to 1st shell (at underarm), ch 3 and complete shell in same shell, ch 3, sc in next shell, (ch 3, shell in next turning ch, ch 3, sc in next turning ch) 4 times; (ch 2, shell in next turning ch)

	4	4
	times	times

Ch 3, sc in next turning ch and work remainder to correspond. Join. There are in rnd

	12	12
	shells	shells

2nd rnd: Sl st in next dc and in sp, ch 3, in same sp make dc, ch 5 and 2 dc; * ch 3, s.o.s., ch 3, in next shell make 2 dc, ch 5 and 2 dc. Repeat from * around. Join. **3rd rnd:** Sl st in next dc and in sp, ch 4, 12 tr in same sp, and complete rnd as for 1st rnd of Skirt. Continue working next 4 rnds as for Skirt. Work each pineapple individually and then work 2 rnds of edging all around as for Skirt. Fasten off.

Work around neck edge as for 2nd rnd of Edging along bottom of Skirt. Make sc with ch's between along back edge to even them up, working 5 ch-8 loops on Right Back edge. Sew buttons to correspond. Cut two 20-inch lengths of velvet ribbon. Pass 1 piece through shells of each armhole (at base of sleeve) and tie into a bow at top.

Cut a 13-inch length of ribbon and pass through shells at neck edge. Sew ends in place. Pass remaining ribbon through Beading and tie in Back.

Pineapple Chair Set & Shade Pull

CHAIR BACK—11½ x 22 inches
ARM PIECES—12 x 12 inches

MATERIALS:

J. & P. COATS or CLARK'S O.N.T. BEST SIX CORD MERCERIZED CROCHET, *Size 30:*

SMALL BALL:
J. & P. COATS —5 balls of White or Ecru, or
OR   7 balls of any color,
CLARK'S O.N.T.—7 balls of White or Ecru, or
                        8 balls of any color.

BIG BALL:
J. & P. COATS —3 balls of White, Ecru, or Cream.
Steel Crochet Hook No. 10 or 11.

CHAIR BACK . . . Starting at center top, ch 8. Join with sl st. **1st row:** Ch 3, in ring make dc, ch 2, 2 dc, ch 3, 2 dc, ch 2 and 2 dc. Ch 5, turn. **2nd row:** In next sp make 2 dc, ch 2 and 2 dc (shell is made), ch 2, in next sp make 2 dc, ch 3 and 2 dc (corner shell is made), ch 2, in same sp make another corner shell, ch 2, shell in next sp. Ch 5, turn. **3rd row:** Shell in sp of shell (shell over shell is made), ch 3, corner shell over corner shell, ch 3, shell in next sp, ch 3,

corner shell over corner shell, ch 3, shell over shell. *Hereafter "shell over shell" will be referred to as "s.o.s."* Ch 5, turn. **4th row:** Make s.o.s. across, having ch-4 between shells and working corner shells as before. Ch 5, turn. **5th row:** Same as previous row, making ch-6 (instead of ch-4) between shells. Ch 5, turn. **6th row:** * S.o.s., ch 6, in next sp make 2 dc, ch 2, 2 dc, ch 3, 2 dc, ch 2 and 2 dc, ch 6. Repeat from * across, ending with s.o.s. Ch 5, turn. **7th row:** * S.o.s., ch 6, shell in next ch-2 sp, ch 2, corner shell in next sp, ch 2, shell in next sp, ch 6. Repeat from * ending with s.o.s. Ch 5, turn. **8th row:** * S.o.s., ch 6, (s.o.s., ch 2, shell in next sp, ch 2) twice, making corner shell as before; s.o.s., ch 6. Repeat from * ending with s.o.s. Ch 5, turn. **9th row:** * S.o.s., ch 6, shell over each of next 5 shells with ch-3 between, making corner shell as before, ch 6. Repeat from * ending with s.o.s. Ch 5, turn.

Hereafter keep all corner shells 2 dc, ch 3 and 2 dc.

10th and 11th rows: Same as previous row, making between the 5 shells at both corners, ch-4 for 10th row and ch-5 for 11th row (instead of ch-3). Ch 5, turn. **12th row:** * (S.o.s., ch 6) twice; in sp of next shell make 2 dc, ch 7 and 2 dc; ch 6, s.o.s., ch 6, in sp of next shell make 2 dc, ch 7 and 2 dc; ch 6, s.o.s., ch 6. Repeat from * ending with s.o.s. Ch 5, turn. **13th row:** * S.o.s., ch 6, s.o.s., ch 2, 20 tr in ch-7 loop, (this is base of pineapple), ch 2, s.o.s., ch 2, 20 tr in next ch-7 loop, ch 2, s.o.s., ch 6. Repeat from * ending with s.o.s. Ch 5, turn. **14th row:** * S.o.s., ch 6, dc in sp of next shell, ch 1, tr in each tr with ch-1 between, ch 1, s.o.s., ch 1, tr in each tr with ch-1 between; ch 1, dc in sp of next shell, ch 6. Repeat from * ending with s.o.s. Ch 5, turn. **15th row:** * S.o.s., ch 5, skip next dc and ch 1, sc in next ch-1 sp between tr's, (ch 3, sc in next sp) 18 times; ch 1, s.o.s., ch 1, skip next tr, sc in next sp, (ch 3, sc in next sp) 18 times; ch 5. Repeat from * ending with s.o.s. Ch 5, turn. **16th row:** * S.o.s., ch 4, sc in next ch-3 loop, (ch 3, sc in next loop) 17 times; ch 1, s.o.s., ch 1, sc in next ch-3 loop, (ch 3, sc in next loop) 17 times; ch 4. Repeat from * ending with s.o.s. Ch 5, turn. **17th row:** * S.o.s., ch 4, sc in next ch-3 loop, (ch 3, sc in next loop) 16 times; ch 1, s.o.s., ch 1, sc in next ch-3 loop, (ch 3, sc in next loop) 16 times; ch 4. Repeat from * ending with s.o.s. Ch 5, turn. **18th and 19th rows:** Same as previous row, having 15 (instead of 16) loops on each pineapple for 18th row, and 14 loops for 19th row. Ch 5, turn. All loops on pineapples are ch-3 loops. **20th row:** * In sp of shell make (2 dc, ch 2) twice and 2 dc; ch 4, sc in next loop, make 13 loops across pineapple, ch 2, in sp of next shell make 2 dc, ch 2, 2 dc, ch 3, 2 dc, ch 2 and 2 dc; ch 2, sc in next loop,

Continued on page 34.

Continued from page 33.

13 loops across pineapple, ch 4. Repeat from * across. In sp of last shell make (2 dc, ch 2) twice and 2 dc. Ch 5, turn.

21st row: * Shell in next sp, ch 2, shell in next sp, ch 4, sc in next loop, make 12 loops across pineapple, ch 3, skip next ch 2, shell in each of next 3 sps with ch 2 between each shell, ch 3, sc in next loop, make 12 loops across pineapple, ch 4. Repeat from * ending with shell in next sp, ch 2, shell in last sp. Ch 5, turn. **22nd row:** * S.o.s., ch 1, shell in next sp, ch 1, s.o.s., ch 4, sc in next loop, make 11 loops across pineapple, ch 4, (s.o.s., shell in next sp) twice; s.o.s., ch 4, sc in next loop, make 11 loops across pineapple, ch 4. Repeat from * ending with s.o.s., ch 1, shell in next sp, s.o.s. Ch 5, turn. **23rd row:** * Shell over each of next 3 shells with ch 2 between shells, ch 4, sc in next loop, make 10 loops across pineapple, ch 4, shell over each of next 5 shells with ch 2 between shells, ch 4, sc in next loop, make 10 loops across pineapple, ch 4. Repeat from * ending with shell over each of next 3 shells with ch 2 between shells. Ch 5, turn. **24th and 25th rows:** Same as previous row, having ch 3 between shells and 9 loops on pineapples for 24th row; and ch 4 between shells and 8 loops on pineapples for 25th row. Ch 5, turn.

26th row: * S.o.s., ch 5, in next shell make 2 dc, ch 7 and 2 dc; ch 5, s.o.s., ch 4, 7 loops across pineapple, ch 4, s.o.s., ch 5, in next shell make 2 dc, ch 7 and 2 dc; ch 5, s.o.s., ch 5, in next shell make 2 dc, ch 7 and 2 dc; ch 5, s.o.s., ch 4, make 7 loops across pineapple, ch 4. Repeat from * ending row to correspond with beginning. Ch 5, turn. Always end each row to correspond with beginning. **27th row:** * S.o.s., ch 4, 20 tr in ch-7 loop, ch 4, s.o.s., ch 4, make 6 loops across pineapple, ch 4, s.o.s., ch 4, 20 tr in ch-7 loop, ch 2, s.o.s., ch 2, 20 tr in ch-7 loop, ch 4, s.o.s., ch 4, make 6 loops across pineapple, ch 4. Repeat from * across. Ch 5, turn. **28th row:** * S.o.s., ch 4, tr in each tr with ch 1 between, ch 4, s.o.s., ch 4, make 5 loops across pine-

apple, ch 4, s.o.s., ch 4, tr in each tr with ch 1 between, ch 1, s.o.s., ch 1, tr in each tr with ch 1 between, ch 4, s.o.s., ch 4, make 5 loops across pineapple, ch 4. Repeat from * across. Ch 5, turn. **29th row:** Work as before, having 18 loops in pineapples on 2nd pineapple row and 4 loops in pineapples on 1st pineapple row. **30th, 31st and 32nd rows:** Work as before, having 1 loop less on each pineapple (on 32nd row, 1 loop remains in pineapples on 1st pineapple row). Ch 5, turn. **33rd row:** * S.o.s., ch 4, 14 loops, ch 4, s.o.s., ch 4, sc in loop, ch 4, s.o.s., ch 4, 14 loops, ch 1, s.o.s., ch 1, 14 loops, ch 4, s.o.s., ch 4, sc in loop, ch 4. Repeat from * across. Ch 5, turn.

34th row: * S.o.s., ch 4, 13 loops, ch 4, s.o.s., ch 1, s.o.s., ch 4, 13 loops, ch 2, in sp of shell make 2 dc, ch 2, 2 dc, ch 3, 2 dc, ch 2 and 2 dc; ch 2, 13 loops, ch 4, s.o.s. Ch 1. Repeat from * across. Ch 5, turn. **35th row:** * S.o.s., ch 4, 12 loops, ch 4, s.o.s., ch 1, shell in next ch-1, ch 1, s.o.s., ch 4, 12 loops, ch 3, skip the ch-2, shell in each of next 3 sps with ch-1 between shells, ch 3, 12 loops, ch 4, s.o.s., ch 1, shell in next ch-1, ch 1. Repeat from * across. Ch 5, turn. **36th row:** S.o.s., * ch 4, 11 loops, ch 4, shell over each of next 3 shells with ch 2 between, ch 4, 11 loops, ch 4, (s.o.s., shell in next sp) twice; s.o.s., ch 4, 11 loops, ch 4, shell over each of next 3 shells with ch 2 between shells. Repeat from * across. Ch 5, turn. **37th, 38th and 39th rows:** Make s.o.s., ch 4, work over 1st pineapple as before and work across in established pattern, ending each row to correspond with beginning. Ch 5, turn. **40th row:** * S.o.s., ch 4, 7 loops across pineapple, ch 4, s.o.s., ch 5, in next shell make 2 dc, ch 7 and 2 dc; ch 5, s.o.s., ch 4, 7 loops across pineapple, ch 5, in next shell make 2 dc, ch 7 and 2 dc; ch 5) twice; s.o.s., ch 4, 7 loops across pineapple, ch 4, s.o.s., ch 5, in next shell make 2 dc, ch 7 and 2 dc; ch 5. Repeat from * across. Ch 5, turn. **41st to 47th rows incl:** Work in pattern across. Ch 5, turn. **48th row:** Place 1st shell over 2nd shell and working over both shells

at once, make a shell in sp of this double shell, ch 4, 13 loops, ch 4, s.o.s., ch 1, s.o.s., and work in pattern across. Ch 5, turn.

To make points, work as follows: **1st row:** S.o.s., ch 4, work loops across pineapple, ch 4, s.o.s. Ch 5, turn. Repeat this row until 1 loop remains on pineapple. Ch 5, turn. **Last row:** S.o.s., tr in loop, shell over next shell, ch 5, turn, sc in sp of last shell made. Fasten off. Attach thread to sp of shell on next pineapple and complete point as before. Work all points in same way.

EDGING . . . 1st rnd: Attach thread in ring at beginning of Chair Back, ch 3, in same place make dc, ch 2 and 2 dc; * ch 2, shell in next ch-5 loop. Repeat from * around, making shell in last ch-5 loop of each point, then ch 2, sc in next ch-1 sp (between shells), ch 2, shell in next ch-5 loop of next point and continue thus around. Join last ch-2 to ch-3. **2nd rnd:** Sl st in next dc and in next sp, ch 8, sc in 5th ch from hook (p made), dc in same sp as last sl st, * ch 3, sc in ch-2 sp between shells, ch 3, in sp of next shell make dc, p and dc. Repeat from * ending with dc in last shell of first point; now make a p, dc in sp of 1st shell of next point, ch 3, sc in next ch-2 sp, in sp of next shell make dc, p and dc; and continue thus around. Join and fasten off.

ARM PIECES . . . Starting at one point, ch 8. Join with sl st. **1st row:** Ch 3, in ring make dc, (ch 2, 2 dc) 3 times. Ch 5, turn. **2nd row:** Shell in next sp, ch 2, corner shell in next sp, ch 2, shell in next sp. Ch 5, turn. **3rd row:** Shell over each shell with ch-3 between, always making corner shell over corner shell. Ch 5, turn. **4th and 5th rows:** Make s.o.s. across, having between shells ch 4 on 4th row and ch 6 on 5th row. Ch 5, turn. Starting with beginning of the 6th row, follow directions for Chair Back, but disregard the phrase "Repeat from * across" in each row, since the Arm Piece is half of Chair Back.

Pineapple Shade Pull

MATERIALS:
J. & P. COATS or CLARK'S O.N.T. BEST SIX CORD MERCERIZED CROCHET, *Size 30* (about 20 yards are required for 1 pull).
Steel Crochet Hook No. 8 or 9.
1 bone ring about ¾ inch in diameter.

1st rnd: Sc closely over bone ring. Sl st in 1st sc. Now work in rows (back and forth). **1st row:** Ch 5, in same place as sl st make 2 dc, ch 2 and 2 dc (shell is made); ch 3, skip 6 sc, in next sc make 2 dc, ch 5 and 2 dc; ch 3, skip 6 sc, in next sc make a shell as before. Ch 5, turn. **2nd row:** Shell in sp of shell (shell over shell is made), ch 3, in ch-5 sp make 15 tr, ch 3, shell over shell. Ch 5, turn. *Hereafter "shell over shell" will be referred to as "s.o.s."* Ch 5, turn. **3rd row:** S.o.s., ch 3, tr in each tr with ch-1 between, ch 3, s.o.s. Ch 5, turn. **4th row:** S.o.s., ch 3, sc in first ch-1 sp, (ch 3, sc

in next sp) 13 times, ch 3, s.o.s. Ch 5, turn. **5th row:** S.o.s., ch 3, skip next ch-3, sc in next loop, (ch 3, sc in next loop) 12 times, ch 3, s.o.s. Ch 5, turn. **6th row:** S.o.s., ch 3, skip next ch-3, sc in next loop, (ch 3, sc in next loop) 11 times, ch 3, s.o.s. Ch 5, turn.

Continue in this manner, having 1 loop less on each row until 1 loop remains. Ch 5, turn. **Last row:** S.o.s., ch 3, sc in loop, ch 3, 2 dc in sp of next shell, ch 1, sc in sp of last complete shell made, ch 1, 2 dc in same shell where last 2 dc were made, ch 5, turn, sc in joining sc (between last 2 shells). Fasten off.

CORD . . . Cut 6 strands of thread, each 1 yard long. Twist these strands tightly. Now double these strands and give them a second twist in the opposite direction. Knot free ends. Sew to pull as in illustration.

Pineapple Doily

Centerpiece measures about 22 inches in diameter

MATERIALS: J. & P. Coats or Clark's O.N.T. Best Six Cord Mercerized Crochet, *Size 30:* **Small Ball:** J. & P. Coats—*8 balls of White or Ecru, or 9 balls of any color, or* Clark's O.N.T.—*12 balls of White or Ecru, or 14 balls of any color* . . . *Steel Crochet Hook No. 10.*

Starting at center, ch 14. Join with sl st to form ring. **1st rnd:** Ch 4, 31 tr in ring. Join with sl st to top of ch-4. **2nd rnd:** Ch 4, tr in next tr, * ch 4, skip 2 tr, tr in next 2 tr. Repeat from * around, ending with ch 4, sl st in top of ch-4. **3rd rnd:** Sc in same place as sl st, sc in next tr, * 6 sc in next loop, sc in next 2 tr. Repeat from * around. Join. **4th rnd:** Sl st in next 4 sc, ch 4, tr in next sc, * ch 8, skip 6 sc, tr in next 2 sc. Repeat from * around. Join. **5th rnd:** Sc in same place as sl st, sc in next tr, * 12 sc in next sp, sc in next 2 tr. Repeat from * around. Join. **6th rnd:** Ch 4, tr in next sc, * ch 6, skip 5 sc, tr in next 2 sc. Repeat from * around. Join. **7th rnd:** Sc in same place as sl st, sc in next tr, * 8 sc in next sp, tr in next 2 tr. Repeat from * around.

Join. **8th rnd:** Sl st in next 4 sc, ch 4, tr in next sc, * ch 8, skip 8 sc, tr in next 2 sc. Repeat from * around. Join. **9th rnd:** Sc in same place as sl st, sc in next tr, 12 sc in each loop around. Join. **10th rnd:** Sl st in next 5 sc, ch 4, tr in next sc, * ch 12, skip 10 sc, tr in next 2 sc. Repeat from * around. Join. **11th rnd:** Sl st in next tr, * 16 sc in next loop, ch 2. Repeat from * around. Join. **12th rnd:** Sl st in next 7 sc, ch 10, d tr in next sc, * ch 9, skip 7 sc on next loop, 3 tr in next sc, ch 2, 3 tr in next sc (shell made), ch 9, skip 7 sc of next loop, d tr in next sc, ch 4, d tr in next sc. Repeat from * around, ending with ch 9, sl st in 6th ch of starting ch-10. **13th rnd:** Sl st in next sp, ch 4, 14 tr in same sp, * ch 7, in sp of next shell make 3 tr, ch 2 and 3 tr (shell made over shell), ch 7, 15 tr in next ch-4 loop. Repeat from * around. Join. **14th rnd:** Ch 5, (tr in next tr, ch 1) 13 times; * tr in next tr, ch 6, shell over shell, ch 6, (tr in next tr, ch 1) 14 times. Repeat from * around. Join. **15th rnd:** Sl st in ch-1 sp, sc in same sp, * (ch 4, sc in next sp) 13 times; ch 5, in sp of next shell

make (3 tr, ch 2) twice and 3 tr; ch 5, sc in next ch-1 sp. Repeat from * around. Join. **16th rnd:** Sl st in next ch, * sc in loop, (ch 4, sc in next loop) 12 times; ch 5, (shell in next ch-2 sp) twice; ch 5. Repeat from * around. Join. **17th rnd:** Sl st in next ch, * sc in loop, (ch 4, sc in next loop) 11 times; ch 5, (shell over shell) twice. Repeat from * around. Join with d tr to first sc.

Pineapples are now worked individually in rows as follows:

First Pineapple: 1st row: Turn work, sl st in 3 tr and in sp, ch 4, turn; in same sp make 2 tr, ch 2 and 3 tr; ch 5, sc in next loop, (ch 4, sc in next loop) 10 times; ch 5, shell over shell. Turn. **2nd row:** Sl st to sp of shell, ch 4 and complete shell in same sp, ch 5, sc in next loop, (ch 4, sc in next loop) 9 times; ch 5, shell over shell. Turn. Repeat the 2nd row, having 1 loop less on each row until 1 loop remains. **Next row:** Shell over shell, ch 5, sc in loop, ch 5, shell over shell, turn. **Following**

Continued on page 44.

RUNNER—page 37

TRAY MAT—page 38

ROUND LUNCHEON SET—page 38

Daisy Pineapples

RUNNER

15 x 40 inches . . . motif measures 2 inches in diameter

MATERIALS:

J. & P. Coats or Clark's O.N.T. Best Six Cord Mercerized Crochet, Size 30:

SMALL BALL:

J. & P. COATS—5 balls of White or Ecru, or 6 balls of any color, or

CLARK'S O.N.T.—7 balls of White or Ecru, or 9 balls of any color, or

BIG BALL:

J. & P. COATS—3 balls of White, Ecru or Cream, or 4 balls of any color, or

Clark's Big Ball Three Cord Mercerized Crochet, Size 30: 2 balls of White, Ecru or Cream, or 3 balls of any color.

Milward's Steel Crochet Hook No. 10.

FIRST MOTIF . . . Starting at center, ch 12. Join with sl st to form ring. **1st rnd:** Ch 4, 31 tr in ring, sl st to 4th ch of ch-4. **2nd rnd:** Sc in same place as sl st, * ch 5, skip 1 tr, sc in next tr. Repeat from * around, ending with ch 2, dc in first sc. **3rd rnd:** Ch 4, holding back on hook the last loop of each tr make 2 tr in loop just formed, thread over and draw through all loops on hook (cluster), * ch 7; make a 3-tr cluster in next loop. Repeat from * around, joining last ch-7 to tip of first cluster (16 clusters). Break off.

SECOND MOTIF . . . Work as for First Motif until 2nd rnd is completed. **3rd rnd:** Ch 4, make a 2-tr cluster in loop just formed, ch 3, sl st in corresponding loop on First Motif; ch 3, make a 3-tr cluster in next ch-5 loop on Second Motif, ch 3, sl st in corresponding loop on First Motif; ch 3, cluster in next ch-5 loop on Second Motif and complete rnd as for First Motif (no more joinings).

Make 3 rows of 14 motifs, joining motifs as Second Motif was joined to First Motif, leaving 2 loops free between joinings.

FILL-IN LACE . . . Ch 1, tr tr in first free loop of motif (following any joining), tr tr in next free loop, * long tr (6 times over hook) in joining, (tr tr in next free loop) twice. Repeat from * around. Sl st in first tr tr. Break off. Fill in all spaces in the same manner.

PINEAPPLE BORDER—First Corner Pineapple . . . With right side facing, skip 3 free loops on any corner motif following joining, mark next loop. With wrong side facing, attach thread to center of marked loop, ch 7, sc in next loop. Ch 4, turn. **1st row:** 10 tr in ch-7 loop, tr where thread was attached. Ch 5, turn. **2nd row:**

Skip first tr, (tr in next tr, ch 1) 10 times; tr in top of ch-4. Ch 6, turn. **3rd row:** Skip first tr, (tr in next tr, ch 2) 10 times; skip 1 ch of turning chain, tr in next ch. Ch 5, turn. **4th row:** Sc in next ch-2 sp, (ch 5, sc in next sp) 10 times. Ch 5, turn. **5th row:** Sc in next loop, (ch 5, sc in next loop) 9 times. Ch 5, turn. **6th row:** Sc in next loop, (ch 5, sc in next loop) 8 times. Ch 5, turn. **7th row:** Sc in next loop, (ch 5, sc in next loop) 7 times. Ch 5, turn. Continue in this manner, having 1 loop less on each row until row ends with sc in next loop, ch 5, sc in next loop. Ch 5, turn. **Next row:** Skip 1 ch of next loop, sc in next ch, ch 5, skip 1 ch, sc in next ch of same loop. Break off.

SECOND CORNER PINEAPPLE . . . With right side facing, skip next loop on same motif, mark next loop. With wrong side facing, attach thread to marked loop, ch 7, sc in next loop, ch 4, sl st in last tr of 1st row of previous pineapple, turn. **1st row:** 6 tr in ch-7 loop, tr where thread was attached. Ch 5, turn. **2nd row:** Skip first tr, (tr in next tr, ch 1) 6 times; tr in top of turning chain below, sl st in corresponding st of previous pineapple, ch 4, sl st in next loop of previous pineapple, turn. **3rd row:** Ch 2, skip next tr, (tr in next tr, ch 2) 6 times; skip 1 ch, tr in next ch. Ch 5, turn. **4th row:** Sc in next ch-2 sp, (ch 5, sc in next sp) 6 times; ch 2, sl st in second turning ch-5 loop on previous pineapple. Ch 2, turn. **5th row:** Sc in next loop, (ch 5, sc in next loop) 6 times. Ch 5, turn. **6th row:** Sc in next loop, (ch 5, sc in next loop) 5 times. Ch 5, turn. Continue in this manner, having 1 loop less on each row and completing pineapple exactly as for First Corner Pineapple. Break off.

THIRD CORNER PINEAPPLE . . . With right side facing, skip next loop of same motif, mark next loop. With wrong side facing, attach thread to marked loop, ch 7, sc in next loop, ch 4, sl st in adjacent st of Second Corner Pineapple. Turn. **1st row:** 10 tr in loop, tr where thread was attached. Ch 5, turn. Complete as for First Corner Pineapple, joining to correspond with previous joinings.

FIRST SIDE PINEAPPLE . . . With right side facing, skip 3 free loops on next motif, mark next loop. With wrong side facing, attach thread to marked loop, ch 7, sc in next loop. Ch 4, turn. **1st row:** 10 tr in loop, tr where thread was attached. Ch 5, turn and complete as for First Corner Pineapple, joining 2 turning chain loops of this pineapple to corresponding loops of adjacent pineapple as before. Make a Side Pineapple on each motif, joining as before. Continue in this manner all around, making

3 corner pineapples on each corner motif and taking care to join last pineapple on both sides.

EDGING . . . **1st rnd:** Attach thread to first free loop on First Corner Pineapple, ch 4, holding back on hook the last loop of each tr make 2 tr in same loop, thread over and draw through all loops on hook (cluster made), (ch 7, make a 3-tr cluster in next free loop) twice; (ch 7, in next ch-5 loop make cluster, ch 7 and cluster) twice; (ch 7, cluster in next loop) 3 times; cluster in next free loop of next pineapple, ch 7, cluster in next loop, (ch 7, in next loop make cluster, ch 7 and cluster) twice; (ch 7, cluster in next loop) twice; * cluster in next free loop on next pineapple, (ch 7, cluster in next free loop) twice; (ch 7, in next free loop make cluster, ch 7 and cluster) twice; (ch 7, cluster in next free loop) 3 times. Repeat from * around, working over corner pineapples as before. Join last cluster with sl st to tip of first cluster. **2nd rnd:** Sl st to center of next loop, * ch 7, sc in next loop. Repeat from * around corner, ending with sc in loop preceding last 2 clusters of Third Corner Pineapple, ** ch 3, tr in next 2 loops, ch 3, sc in next loop, (ch 7, sc in next loop) 6 times. Repeat from ** around, working over corner pineapples as before and ending with ch 3, tr in last ch-7 loop, sl st in center of first loop. **3rd rnd:** (Ch 9, sc in next loop) 22 times; * ch 3, tr in next 2 tr, ch 3, sc in next ch-7 loop, (ch 9, sc in next loop) 5 times. Repeat from * around, working over corners as before and ending with ch 3, tr in last tr, sl st in center of first loop. **4th rnd:** Ch 5, sc in next loop, (ch 11, sc in next loop) 6 times; sc in next loop, (ch 11, sc in next loop) 6 times; sc in next loop, (ch 11, sc in next loop) 6 times; * ch 1, tr in next 2 tr, ch 1, sc in next loop, (ch 11, sc in next loop) 4 times. Repeat from * around, working over corners as before and ending with ch 1, tr in last tr, sl st in 4th st of ch-5. **5th rnd:** Sl st to center of next ch-11 loop, sc in same loop, * (ch 13, sc in next loop) 5 times; sc in next loop. Repeat from * 2 more times; ** (ch 13, sc in next loop) 3 times; sc in next loop. Repeat from ** around, working over corners as before. Join and break off.

Work Fill-in laces between motifs and pineapples as follows: Ch 1, tr tr in free loop of motif following pineapple, tr tr in next loop, long tr in joining, tr tr in next loop on next motif, tr tr in next loop, tr tr at end of 1st row of pineapple, tr tr at end of next row on same pineapple, long tr in joining, make tr tr at end of 2nd and 1st rows of next pineapple. Sl st in first tr tr. Break off. Fill in remaining spaces in the same way. Starch lightly and press.

Pineapple Wheel

Doily measures 12 inches in diameter

MATERIALS:

J. & P. Coats or Clark's O.N.T. Best Six Cord Mercerized Crochet, Size 30:

SMALL BALL:
J. & P. COATS—2 balls of No. 9 Yellow, or
CLARK'S O.N.T.—3 balls of No. 9 Yellow, or

BIG BALL:
J. & P. COATS—1 ball of No. 9 Yellow, or

Clark's Big Ball Three Cord Mercerized Crochet, Size 30: 1 ball of No. 9 Yellow, and

J. & P. Coats or Clark's O.N.T. Pearl Cotton, Size 5: 1 ball of No. 48 Hunter's Green.

Milward's Steel Crochet Hook Nos. 7 and 10.

Starting at center with Yellow and No. 10 hook, ch 10. Join with sl st to form ring. **1st rnd:** Ch 2, 24 half dc in ring. Join with sl st to first half dc. **2nd rnd:** Ch 4, * dc in next half dc, ch 1. Repeat from * around. Join to 3rd ch of ch-4. **3rd rnd:** Sl st in next sp, sc in same sp, * ch 3, sc in next sp. Repeat from * around. Join. **4th rnd:** Sl st to center of next loop, sc in same loop, * ch 3, sc in next loop. Repeat from * around. Join. **5th rnd:** Sl st to center of next loop, sc in same loop, * ch 4, sc in next loop. Repeat from * around. Join. **6th rnd:** Sl st to center of next loop, ch 4, tr in next loop, * ch 7, holding back on hook the last

loop of each tr make tr in each of next 2 loops, thread over and draw through all loops on hook (joint tr made). Repeat from * around. Join and break off. **7th rnd:** Attach Green Pearl Cotton to any sp and, using No. 7 hook, make 6 sc in same sp, * ch 27, sc in 2nd ch from hook and in each ch across, sc in side of last sc made in sp, 6 sc in next sp. Repeat from * around. Join and break off (12 spokes). **8th rnd:** Using No. 10 hook, attach Yellow to 7th sc from center on any spoke, * ch 12, sc in 6th ch from hook (picot made); ch 6, sl st in base of corresponding sc on next spoke, ch 2, holding chain in back of spoke, sl st in same sc. Repeat from * around. Join. **9th rnd:** Sl st to next picot, sl st in picot, ch 5, 5 d tr in same picot, * ch 6, skip 4 sc on spoke, sl st in base of next sc, ch 2, holding chain in back of spoke, sl st in same sc, ch 6, 6 d tr in next picot. Repeat from * around. Join to 5th ch of ch-5.

10th rnd: Ch 5, (tr in next d tr, ch 1) 4 times; tr in next d tr, * ch 6, skip 2 sc on spoke, sl st in base of next sc, ch 2, holding chain in back of spoke, sl st in same sc, ch 6, (tr in next d tr, ch 1) 5 times; tr in next d tr. Repeat from * around. Join to 4th ch of ch-5. **11th rnd:** Sl st in next sp, sc in same sp, * (ch 5, sc in next sp) 4 times; ch 5, skip next tr, sc in next ch, ch 5, skip 2 sc on spoke, sl st in base of next sc, ch 2, holding chain in back of spoke sl st in same sc, ch 5, skip 5 ch, sc in next ch, ch 5, sc in next sp. Repeat from * around, ending with sc in chain, ch 2, dc in first sc. **12th**

rnd: Sl st in loop formed by ch 2 and dc, ch 4, holding back on hook the last loop of each tr make 2 tr in same loop, thread over and draw through all loops on hook (cluster made); * (ch 3, 3-tr cluster in next loop) 5 times; ch 3, skip 2 sc on spoke, sl st in base of next sc, ch 2, holding chain in back of spoke, sl st in same sc, ch 3, skip next sp, cluster in next loop. Repeat from * around. Join. **13th rnd:** Sl st in next sp, ch 4, 2-tr cluster in same sp, * (ch 3, cluster in next sp) 4 times; ch 5, skip 2 sc on spoke, sl st in base of next sc, ch 2, holding chain in back of spoke, sl st in same sc, ch 5, skip next sp, cluster in next sp. Repeat from * around. Join. **14th rnd:** Sl st in next sp, ch 4, 2-tr cluster in same sp, * (ch 3, cluster in next sp) 3 times; ch 10, sc in tip of next spoke, ch 10, skip next sp, cluster in next sp. Repeat from * around. Join. **15th rnd:** Sl st in next sp, ch 4, 2-tr cluster in same sp, * (ch 3, cluster in next sp) twice; (ch 10, sc in next loop) twice; ch 10, cluster in next sp. Repeat from * around. Join. **16th rnd:** Sl st in next sp, ch 4, 2-tr cluster in same sp, * ch 3, cluster in next sp, (ch 10, sc in next loop) 3 times; ch 10, cluster in next sp. Repeat from * around. Join and break off.

LEAVES . . . With Green and No. 7 hook, attach thread between any 2 clusters, sc in same sp, (ch 7, sc in 2nd ch from hook and next 2 ch, half dc in next 3 ch, sc in same sp) 3 times. Break off. Make a leaf in each sp between clusters around. Starch lightly and press.

Daisy Pineapples

Round Luncheon Set

MATERIALS:

J. & P. Coats or Clark's O.N.T. Best Six Cord Mercerized Crochet, Size 30:

SMALL BALL:
J. & P. COATS—4 balls of White or Ecru, or 5 balls of any color, or
CLARK'S O.N.T.—6 balls of White or Ecru, or 8 balls of any color, or

BIG BALL:
J. & P. COATS—2 balls of White, Ecru or Cream, or 3 balls of any color, or

Clark's Big Ball Three Cord Mercerized Crochet, Size 30: 2 balls of White, Ecru or Cream, or 3 balls of any color.

Milward's Steel Crochet Hook No. 10.

Centerpiece measures 15 inches across center; each Place Mat 13 inches.

CENTERPIECE . . . Make 3 rows of 3 motifs as for Runner, joining motifs and making fill-in laces to correspond.

BORDER . . Complete as for Runner.

PLACE MAT (Make 2) . . . Make 2 rows of 2 motifs as for Runner, joining motifs and making fill-in laces to correspond.

BORDER . . . Make 3 corner pineapples on each motif as for Runner, joining First Pineapple of each corner to Third Pineapple of previous corner in the same way that the Side Pineapple of the Runner was joined to Third Pineapple of corner.

EDGING . . . Attach thread to first free loop on corner pineapple, ch 4 and complete a cluster in same loop, * (ch 7, cluster in next free loop) twice; (ch 7, in next ch-5 loop make cluster, ch 7 and cluster) twice; (ch 7, cluster in next loop) 3 times; cluster in next free loop of next pineapple, ch 7, cluster in next loop, (ch 7, in next loop make cluster, ch 7 and cluster) twice; (ch 7, cluster in next loop) twice; cluster in next free loop of next pineapple, (ch 7, cluster in next loop) twice; (ch 7, in next loop make cluster, ch 7 and cluster) twice; (ch 7, cluster in next loop) 3 times; cluster in next loop of next pineapple. Repeat from *

around. Join. Complete edging over each group of corner pineapples to correspond with corner groups of the Runner.

Tray Mat 16 x 23½ inches

MATERIALS:

J. & P. Coats or Clark's O.N.T. Best Six Cord Mercerized Crochet, Size 30:

SMALL BALL:
J. & P. COATS—3 balls of White, or Ecru, or 4 balls of any color, or
CLARK' O.N.T.—4 balls of White or Ecru, or 5 balls of any color, or

BIG BALL:
J. & P. COATS—2 balls of White, Ecru or Cream, or 3 balls of any color, or

Clark's Big Ball Three Cord Mercerized Crochet, Size 30, 2 balls of White, Ecru or Cream, or any color.

Milward's Steel Crochet Hook No. 10.

Make 4 rows of 7 motifs as for the Runner, joining motifs and making fill-in laces to correspond.

BORDER . . . Complete as for the Runner.

Pineapple Lamp Shades

MATERIALS—Lily Antique Bedspread Cotton (Art. 59):—1-sk. White, Cream or Ecru. Crochet hook size 10. Lamp shade frames 4¾″ across top. 1-yd. sateen in desired color for lining and ruching.

Ch 180, sl st in 1st st. Ch 5, dc in next 3d st, (ch 2, dc in next 3d st) repeated around. Ch 2, sl st in 3d st of 1st 5-ch (60 sps). ROW 2—(Ch 13, sc in next 3d dc) repeated around (20 lps). ROW 3—Sl st to center of next lp, ch 4, dc in same st, (ch 1, dc) 4 times in same st, * ch 4, dc in one lp of center st of next lp, (ch 1, dc) 5 times in same st. Repeat from * around. Ch 4, sl st in 3d st of 1st 4-ch, sl st up to center 1-ch sp. ROW 4—Ch 4, dc in same st, (ch 1, dc) 4 times in same st, (ch 6, a shell in one lp of center 1-ch of next shell) repeated around and join to 3d st of 1st 4-ch. ROW 5—Sl st to center of 1st shell, ch 10, dc in same st, * ch 6, dc in 6-ch lp between shells, ch 6, sc in next shell, ch 6, dc in next 6-ch between shells, ch 6, (dc, ch 7, dc) in center sp of next shell. Repeat from * around. Join final 6-ch to 3d st of 1st 10-ch, sl st in next 7-ch lp. ROW 6—Ch 7, 3 dtr in same 7-ch lp, holding back the last lp of each dtr on hook, yarn over and pull thru all 4 lps on hook at once for a Cluster, * ch 6, (tr, ch 6, tr) in same lp, ch 6, a 4-dtr-Cluster in same lp, ch 6, sk next dc, tr in next sp, ch 2, a 3-tr-Cluster in next sc, ch 2, tr in next lp, ch 6, a 4-dtr-Cluster in 7-ch tip of next point. Repeat from * around. Ch 6, sl st in 1st Cluster. Sl st to next tr. ROW 7—Ch 5, * 9 tr in next 6-ch lp, 1 tr in next tr, ch 7, sk next large Cluster, tr in next lp, ch 2, a 3-tr-Cluster in next 2-ch sp, ch 2, a Cluster in next sp, ch 2, 1 tr in next sp, ch 7, sk Cluster, tr in next tr. Repeat from * around. Join final 7-ch to 1st 5-ch on pineapple. ROW 8—Ch 9, turn, tr in next sp, * (ch 2, a 3-tr-Cluster in next sp) 3 times, ch 2, 1 tr in next sp, ch 4, tr in next tr, (ch 1, tr in next tr) 10 times, ch 4, tr in next sp. Repeat from * around. Join final 1-ch to 5th st of 1st 9-ch lp. ROW 9—Ch 1, turn, sc in last 1-ch sp, ch 3, dc in same sp, * ch 3, sc in next 1-ch sp, (ch 6, sc in next sp) 7 times, ch 3, a 2-dc-Cluster in next sp, ch 4, sk next tr, tr in next 2-ch sp, (ch 2, a 3-tr-Cluster in next sp) twice, ch 2, tr in next sp, ch 4, a 2-dc-Cluster in 1st 1-ch sp on pineapple. Repeat from * around. End with 4-ch, sl st in top of 1st dc-Cluster. ROW 10—Ch 3, turn, dc in same st, * ch 6, sk next tr, tr in next 2-ch sp, ch 2, a 3-tr-Cluster in next 2-ch sp, ch 2, tr in next sp, ch 6, a 2-dc-Cluster in 2-dc-Cluster on pineapple, ch 3, sc in next 6-ch lp, (ch 6, sc in next lp) repeated across to 2d lp from end, ch 3, a 2-dc-Cluster in end Cluster. Repeat from * around. End with ch 3, sl st in 1st Cluster. ROW 11—Ch 3, turn, dc in same st, * ch 3, sc in next lp, (ch 6, sc in next lp) repeated across to 2d from end, ch 3, a 2-dc-Cluster in end Cluster, ch 6, tr in next Cluster, (ch 2, tr) 3 times in same st, ch 6, a 2-dc-Cluster in next dc-Cluster. Repeat from * around, ending with ch 6, sl st in 1st Cluster. ROW 12—Ch 3, turn, dc in same st, * ch 6, dc in next tr, ch 2, dc in next tr, ch 2, dc in next sp, (ch 2, dc in next tr)

twice, ch 6, a 2-dc-Cluster in next dc-Cluster, ch 3, sc in next lp, (ch 6, sc in next lp) 4 times, ch 3, a 2-dc-Cluster in next Cluster. Repeat from * around, ending with 3-ch, sl st in 1st Cluster. ROW 13—Ch 3, turn, dc in same st, * ch 3, sc in next lp, (ch 6, sc in next lp) 3 times, ch 3, a 2-dc-Cluster in next Cluster, ch 6, dc in next dc, ch 2, dc in next dc, ch 2, (dc, ch 2, dc) in next dc, (ch 2, dc in next dc) twice, ch 6, a 2-dc-Cluster in next dc-Cluster. Repeat from * around. End with ch 6, sl st in 1st Cluster. ROW 14—Ch 5, turn, tr in same st, * ch 6, dc in next dc, (ch 3, dc in next dc) 5 times, ch 6, a 2-tr-Cluster in next Cluster, ch 3, sc in next lp, (ch 7, sc in next lp) twice, ch 3, a 2-tr-Cluster in next Cluster. Repeat from * around. End with ch 3, sl st in 1st Cluster. ROW 15—Ch 5, turn, tr in same st, * ch 3, sc in next lp, ch 7, sc in next lp, ch 3, a 2-tr-Cluster in next Cluster, ch 7, dc in next dc, (ch 6, sc in 2 lps of 5th ch st from hook for a p, ch 1, dc in next dc) 5 times, ch 7, a 2-tr-Cluster in next Cluster. Repeat from * around. Join final 7-ch to 1st Cluster. ROW 16—Ch 5, turn, 1 tr in same st, * ch 8. tr in next dc, (ch 7, p, ch 3, tr in next dc) 5 times, ch 8, a 2-tr-Cluster in next Cluster, ch 4, sc in next lp, ch 4, a 2-tr-Cluster in next Cluster. Repeat from * around. Join final 4-ch to 1st Cluster. ROW 17—Ch 5, turn, 1 tr in same st, * ch 1, a 2-tr-Cluster in next Cluster, ch 8, tr in next tr, (ch 8, p, ch 4, tr in next tr) 5 times, ch 8, a 2-tr-Cluster in next Cluster. Repeat from * around. Join final 8-ch to 1st Cluster. ROW 18—Ch 5 for a tr, turn, * ch 8, tr in next tr, (ch 9, tr in next tr) 5 times, ch 8, tr between next 2 Clusters. Repeat from * around. Join final 8-ch to 5th st of 1st 13-ch. ROW 19—Sl st in next ch st, ch 4, dc in next 2d st, (ch 1, dc in next 2d st) repeated around. Join final 1-ch to 3d st of 1st 4-ch. ROW 20—Ch 1, turn, sc in last 1-ch sp, (ch 3, sc in next 1-ch sp) repeated around. Cut 6″ long, thread to a needle and fasten off on back.

Lay right-side-down in a true circle on a cloth stretched on a board or table, and pin down, stretching several inches until center opening is the same size as top of frame. Pat crochet with a pad of cloth dipped in thick, hot starch. Press thru a cloth until starch is partly set, loosen from cloth, then lay flat until dry and stiff. Make a 2d shade.

RUCHING—With pinking shears, cut 4 strips 2″ wide across width of sateen. Starch remaining cloth very stiff, pressing flat. Cut 2 pieces to fit crochet. Cover shade frames with parchment or thin poster card, extending it ¼″ above top wire. Holding crochet and lining tog. slip them over frame so that 1st Row is ¼″ to ½″ below top of card and tack this top edge in place. Press tip of each pineapple in against shade and tack to bottom edge of frame,—forming ripples between pineapples. Trim bottom edge of lining ⅛″ shorter than crochet. Gather two strips of ruching thru center and sew around top of shade. Repeat for 2d shade.

Pineapple Vanity Set

MATERIALS—Lily Antique Bedspread Cotton (Art. 59) :—
1-sk. White, Cream or Ecru. Crochet hook size 10.

DOILY—(Size—18")—Ch 8, sl st in 1st st. Ch 1, 12 sc in ring, sl st in back lp of 1st sc. Ch 5, 2 tr in same st, holding back the last lp of each tr on hook, thread over and pull thru all 3 lps at once for a Cluster, (ch 6, a 3-tr-Cluster in back lp of next sc) 11 times, ch 3, dc in top of 1st Cluster. ROW 2— (Ch 9, sc in next lp) 12 times. ROW 3—Sl st to center st of next lp, ch 4, dc in same st, (ch 1, dc) 4 times in same st, * dc in one lp of center st of next 9-ch lp, (ch 1, dc) 5 times in same st. Repeat from * around, sl st in 3d st of 1st 4-ch, sl st to center 1-ch sp of 1st shell. ROW 4—Ch 4, dc in same st, (ch 1, dc) 4 times in same st, * ch 2, dc in one lp of center 1-ch of next shell, (ch 1, dc) 5 times in same st. Repeat from * around. Ch 2, sl st in 3d st of 1st 4-ch. Repeat Row 4 but make 4-ch between shells, then repeat again with 6-ch between shells. ROW 7—Sl st to center of next shell, ch 10, dc in same place, * ch 7, sc in 6-ch between shells, ch 7, (dc, ch 7, dc) in center of next shell. Repeat from * around. Join final 7-ch to 3d st of 1st 10-ch. ROW 8—Ch 7, a 3-dtr-Cluster in next 7-ch lp, * ch 6, (tr, ch 6, tr) in same lp, ch 6, a 4-dtr-Cluster in same lp, ch 4, a 4-dtr-Cluster in next point. Repeat from * around. End with ch 2, hdc in top of 1st Cluster. ROW 9—Ch 10, * 1 tr in next tr, 9 tr in next sp, 1 tr in next tr, ch 7, dc in 4-ch between Clusters, ch 7. Repeat from * around. Join final 7-ch to 3d st of 1st 10-ch. ROW 10—Sl st up to 1st tr, ch 6, tr in next tr, (ch 1, tr in next tr) 9 times, * ch 5, tr in next tr, (ch 1, tr in next tr) 10 times. Repeat from * around. Join final 5-ch to 5th st of 1st 6-ch. PINEAPPLE —Sc in next 1-ch, ** (ch 6, sc in next 1-ch sp) 8 times, ch 3,

dc in end sp. * Ch 6, turn, sc in next lp, (ch 6, sc in next lp) repeated across to 2d from end, ch 3, dc in end lp. Repeat from * 3 times. Ch 7, turn, sc in next lp, (ch 7, sc in next lp) twice, ch 3, tr in end lp. Make 2 more rows with 7-ch lps. Ch 8, turn, sc in next lp. Cut 3" long. Join again with 1 sc between 1st 2 tr of next pineapple and repeat from ** until 12 pineapples are completed.

EDGE—Make 9 sc in lp at tip of one pineapple, * (4 sc in next sp) 8 times, 5 sc in next lp, (4 sc in next sp on next pineapple) twice, ch 5, sl st back in 8th sc up side of previous pineapple, ch 1, 5 sc over 5-ch, sl st in last sc on pineapple, (4 sc in next sp) 6 times, 9 sc in next (tip) lp. Repeat from * around. ROW 2—Sl st in 1st 5 sc, ch 7 for a dtr, * ch 7, sc in 2 lps of 5th ch st from hook for a p, ch 3, dtr in next 5th sc, (ch 7, p, ch 3, dtr in next 8th sc) twice, dtr in next 8th sc on next pineapple, (ch 7, p, ch 3, dtr in next 8th sc) twice, ch 7, p, ch 3, dtr in center sc at tip of point, ch 7, p, ch 10, p, ch 3, dtr in same sc. Repeat from * around. Join final p-lp to 7th st of 1st one. ROW 3—Ch 14, p, ch 3, dtr in next dtr, ch 7, p, ch 3, dtr in next dtr, * sk 2 ps in angle, dtr in next dtr, (ch 7, p, ch 3, dtr in next dtr) twice, ch 7, p, ch 3, dtr in center st of next lp, ch 7, p, ch 10, p, ch 3, dtr in same st, (ch 7, p, ch 3, dtr in next dtr) 3 times. Repeat from * around and join to 7th st of 1st lp. ROW 4—Work another row in same way except make the large lp at tip of each point of (ch 7, p) 3 times and ch 3. At end of row, cut thread 6" long, thread to a needle and fasten off on back.

Lay Doily right-side-down on a true circle, stretch several inches and pin down each lp around edge. Steam and press dry thru a cloth. Make a 2d Doily.

Pineapple Centerpiece

MATERIALS: J. & P. Coats or
Clark's O.N.T. Best Six Cord Mer-
cerized Crochet, *Size 30:* **Small
Ball:** J. & P. Coats—*4 balls of White
or Ecru, or 5 balls of any color, or*
Clark's O.N.T.—*5 balls of White or
Ecru, or 8 balls of any color . . . Steel
Crochet Hook No. 10.*

Centerpiece measures 20 inches in diameter

Starting at center, ch 10. Join with
sl st to form ring. **1st rnd:** Ch 3, 21 dc
in ring. Sl st to top of ch-3. **2nd rnd:**
Ch 5, * dc in next dc, ch 2. Repeat
from * around. Sl st in 3rd ch of ch-5
(22 sps). **3rd rnd:** Sc in next sp,
* draw loop on hook out to measure
⅜ inch, thread over and draw loop
through, insert hook between single
and double loops and draw a loop
through, thread over and draw through
2 loops on hook (knot st made), make
another knot st, sc in next sp. Repeat
from * around, ending with 2 knot sts,
sl st in 1st sc. **4th to 7th rnds incl:**
* Make 2 knot sts, sc under double
loop of next knot st (to the right of
the knot), sc under double loop of
next knot st (to the left of the same
knot). Repeat from * around (22
loops). Make 1 knot st after the
7th rnd is completed. **8th rnd:** * Sc
under double loop of next knot st (to
the right of next knot), ch 3, sc to
left of same knot, ch 6. Repeat from *
around. Join last ch-6 to 1st sc (22
ch-3 loops). **9th rnd:** Sl st in next
loop, ch 3, in same loop make dc,
ch 2 and 2 dc (shell made), * ch 6,
in next ch-3 loop make 2 dc, ch 2

and 2 dc (another shell made). Repeat
from * around. Join to top of ch-3.
10th rnd: Sl st in next dc and in next
sp, ch 3, in same sp make dc, ch 5
and 2 dc, * ch 6; in next ch-2 sp
make 2 dc, ch 2 and 2 dc; ch 6, in
next ch-2 sp make 2 dc, ch 5 and
2 dc. Repeat from * around. Join.

11th rnd: Sl st in next dc and in
next sp, ch 4, 12 tr in same sp, * ch 5,
in next ch-2 make 2 dc, ch 2 and 2 dc,
ch 5, 13 tr in next ch-5. Repeat from *
around, ending with ch 5. Join. **12th
rnd:** Ch 5, tr in next tr, (ch 1, tr in
next tr) 11 times; * ch 3, shell in sp
of next shell, ch 3, tr in next tr, (ch 1,
tr in next tr) 12 times. Repeat from *
around. Join to 4th st of ch-5. **13th
rnd:** Sl st in 1st ch-1 sp, sc in same
sp, * (ch 3, sc in next ch-1 sp)
11 times; ch 3, shell over shell, ch 3,
sc in next ch-1 sp. Repeat from *
around, ending with ch 3, sc in 1st
ch-3 loop. **14th rnd:** (Ch 3, sc in next
loop) 10 times; * ch 3, shell over
shell, (ch 3, sc in next ch-3 loop)
11 times. Repeat from * around, ending as in 13th rnd. **15th rnd:** (Ch 3,
sc in next loop) 9 times; * ch 3, in
ch-2 of next shell make (2 dc, ch 2)
twice and 2 dc; (ch 3, sc in next loop)
10 times. Repeat from * around, ending as before. **16th rnd:** (Ch 3, sc in
next loop) 8 times; * ch 3, shell in
next ch-2, ch 2, shell in next ch-2,
(ch 3, sc in next loop) 9 times. Repeat from * around, ending as before.
17th rnd: (Ch 3, sc in next loop)
7 times; * ch 3, shell over next shell,
ch 1, shell in next ch-2 sp, ch 1, shell
over next shell, (ch 3, sc in next loop)
8 times. Repeat from * around, ending

as before. **18th rnd:** (Ch 3, sc in next
loop) 6 times; * (ch 3, shell over
next shell) 3 times; (ch 3, sc in next
loop) 7 times. Repeat from * around,
ending as before. **19th rnd:** (Ch 3, sc
in next loop) 5 times; * ch 3, shell
over next shell, (ch 4, shell over next
shell) twice; (ch 3, sc in next loop)
6 times. Repeat from * around.
20th rnd: (Ch 3, sc in next loop)
4 times; * ch 3, shell over next shell,
ch 5, in next shell make 2 dc, ch 5
and 2 dc; ch 5, shell over next shell,
(ch 3, sc in next loop) 5 times. Repeat
from * around. **21st rnd:** (Ch 3, sc
in next loop) 3 times; * ch 3, shell
over next shell, ch 3, 14 tr in next
shell, ch 3, shell over next shell, (ch 3,
sc in next loop) 4 times. Repeat
from * around. **22nd rnd:** (Ch 3, sc
in next loop) twice; * ch 3, shell over
next shell, ch 3, tr in next tr, (ch 1,
tr in next tr) 13 times; ch 3, shell
over next shell, (ch 3, sc in next loop)
3 times. Repeat from * around. **23rd
rnd:** Ch 3, sc in next loop, * ch 3,
shell over shell, (ch 3, sc in next
ch-1 sp) 13 times; ch 3, shell over
shell, (ch 3, sc in next loop) twice.
Repeat from * around. **24th rnd:**
* Ch 4, shell over shell, (ch 3, sc in
next loop) 12 times; ch 3, shell over
shell, ch 4, sc in next loop. Repeat
from * around, ending with ch 4,
sl st in sc. **25th rnd:** Sl st to sp of
shell, ch 3, in same sp make dc, ch 2
and 2 dc; * (ch 3, sc in next loop)
11 times; (ch 3, shell over shell)
twice. Repeat from * around, ending
with ch 3. Join. **26th rnd:** Sl st to sp
of shell, ch 3, in same sp make dc,
Continued on page 44.

Pineapple Petals

Doily measures 11 inches in diameter

MATERIALS:

J. & P. Coats or Clark's O.N.T. Best Six Cord Mercerized Crochet, Size 20:

SMALL BALL:
  J. & P. COATS—2 balls of White or Ecru, or
  CLARK'S O.N.T.—3 balls of White or Ecru, or

BIG BALL:
  J. & P. COATS—2 balls of White, Ecru or Cream, or

Clark's Big Ball Three Cord Mercerized Crochet, Size 20: 2 balls of White, Ecru or Cream.

Milward's Steel Crochet Hook No. 9.

Starting at center, ch 12. Join with sl st to form ring. **1st rnd:** Ch 3, 31 dc in ring. Join to 3rd ch of ch-3. **2nd rnd:** Ch 8, * skip 3 dc, dc in next dc, ch 5. Repeat from * around. Join to 3rd ch of ch-8. **3rd rnd:** Ch 3, * 6 dc in next sp, dc in next dc. Repeat from * around. Join. **4th rnd:** Ch 5, holding back on hook the last loop of each d tr make 2 d tr in same place as sl st, thread over and draw through all loops on hook (cluster made); * ch 12, sc in 6th ch from hook (picot made), ch 6, skip 6 dc, make a 3-d tr cluster in next dc. Repeat from * around. Join to tip of first cluster. **5th rnd:** Sl st in next 6 ch and in picot, ch 4, 9 tr in same picot, * ch 8, 10 tr in next picot. Repeat from * around. Join. **6th rnd:** Ch 5, (tr in next tr, ch 1) 8 times; tr in next tr, * ch 4, tr in next sp, ch 4, (tr in next tr, ch 1) 9 times. Repeat from * around. Join. **7th rnd:** Sl st in next sp, sc in same sp, * (ch 3, sc in next sp) 8 times; ch 4, skip next sp, 2 dc in next tr, ch 4, skip next sp, sc in

Continued on page 44.

43

PINEAPPLE PETALS
Continued from page 43.

next sp. Repeat from * around. Join. **8th rnd:** Sl st in next loop, sc in same loop, * (ch 3, sc in next loop) 7 times; ch 4, skip next sp, sc in next loop. Repeat from * around. Join. **9th rnd:** Sl st in next loop, sc in same loop, * (ch 3, sc in next loop) 6 times; ch 4, dc in next dc, ch 1, dc in next dc, ch 4, skip next sp, sc in next loop. Repeat from * around. Join. **10th rnd:** Sl st in next loop, sc in same loop, * (ch 3, sc in next loop) 5 times; ch 4, dc in next dc, dc in ch-1 sp, dc in next dc, ch 4, skip next sp, sc in next loop. Repeat from * around. Join. **11th rnd:** Sl st in next loop, sc in same loop, * (ch 3, sc in next loop) 4 times; ch 4, 2 dc in each of next 3 dc, ch 4, skip next sp, sc in next loop. Repeat from * around. Join. **12th rnd:** Sl st in next loop, sc in same loop, * (ch 3, sc in next loop) 3 times; ch 4, 2 dc in each of next 6 dc, ch 4, skip next sp, sc in next loop. Repeat from * around. Join. **13th rnd:** Sl st in next loop, sc in same loop, * (ch 3, sc in next loop) twice; ch 4, dc in next dc, 2 dc in each of next 10 dc, dc in next dc, ch 4, skip next sp, sc in next loop. Repeat from * around. Join. **14th rnd:** Sl st in next loop, sc in same loop, * ch 3, sc in next loop, ch 4, dc in each dc across, ch 4, skip next sp, sc in next loop. Repeat from * around. Join. **15th rnd:** Sl st to center of loop, sc in same loop, * ch 5, dc in each dc across, ch 5, skip next sp, sc in next loop. Repeat from * around. Join.

Now work pineapple individually as follows: **1st row:** Ch 7, dc in each dc across. Ch 4, dc in next sc. Ch 7, turn. **2nd and 3rd rows:** Skip first dc, dc in each dc across, ch 4, skip 4 ch, dc in next ch. Ch 7, turn. **4th and 5th rows:** Dec 1 dc—*to dec 1 dc. work off 2 dc as 1 dc*—dc in each dc across to within last 2 dc, dec 1 dc, ch 4, skip 3 ch, dc in next ch. Ch 7, turn. **6th, 7th and 8th rows:** Skip first dc, dec 2 dc—*to dec 2 dc, work off 3 dc as 1 dc*—dc in each dc across to within last 3 dc, dec 2 dc, ch 4, skip 3 ch, dc in next ch. Ch 7, turn. **9th row:** Skip first dc, dec 2 dc, dc in next dc, dec 1 dc, ch 4, skip 3 ch, dc in next ch. Ch 7, turn. **10th row:** Skip first dc, dec 2 dc, ch 4, skip 4 ch, dc in next ch. Ch 10, turn. Skip first sp and 4 ch on next sp, sl st in next ch. Break off.

NEXT PINEAPPLE . . . Attach thread to same sc on 15th rnd, and complete as before. Make remaining pineapples in same way.

EDGING . . . Attach thread to the first sp on the side of any pineapple, 3 sc in same sp, * (in next sp make sc, dc, ch 4, sc in 4th ch from hook —picot made—dc and sc) 9 times; in next sp make sc, 6 dc, picot, 5 dc and sc; (in next sp make sc, dc, picot, dc and sc) 9 times; 3 sc in each of next 2 sps. Repeat from * around. Join and break off. Starch lightly and press.

PINEAPPLE DOILY
Continued from page 35.

row: Shell over shell, ch 1, shell over shell, turn. **Last row:** Sl st to sp of shell, shell in ch-1 sp, sl st in sp of next shell. Break off.

Second Pineapple: Attach thread to sp of next free shell on last rnd, make shell over shell and complete as for First Pineapple. Work all pineapples in this manner. At end of last pineapple do not break off but work in rnds as follows: **1st rnd:** Sl st to end of shell, ch 8, (tr in end of next shell, ch 4) 8 times; * holding back on hook the last loop of each tr make tr in end of next 2 shells, skip 2 shells, tr in end of next 2 shells, thread over and draw through all loops on hook; ch 4, (tr in end of next shell, ch 4) 9 times; in tip of pineapple make tr, ch 4 and tr; (ch 4, tr in end of next shell) 9 times; ch 4. Repeat from * around, ending with ch 4, sl st in 4th st of starting chain. **2nd rnd:** Sl st in loop, ch 13, skip next loop, tr in next loop, ch 8, skip next loop, tr in next loop, ch 8, skip 2 tr, d tr in next tr, * d tr in corresponding tr on next pineapple, ch 8, skip 2 sps, tr in next sp, (ch 8, skip 1 sp, tr in next sp) twice; ch 8, skip 1 sp, 5 dc in sp at tip of pineapple, (ch 8, skip 1 sp, tr in next sp) 3 times; ch 8, skip 2 sps, d tr in next tr. Repeat from * around. Join. **3rd rnd:** Ch 8, tr in next loop, * ch 4, tr in next tr, ch 8, d tr in next tr, ch 4, in loop formed by next 2 d tr make tr tr, ch 4 and tr tr; ch 4, d tr in next tr, turn; in ch-4 loop between tr tr's make 4 d tr, ch 2, 5 d tr, ch 2 and 4 d tr; sl st in next d tr, sl st in next 4 ch of ch-8, turn. Holding back on hook the last loop of each d tr make d tr in next 4 d tr, thread over and draw through all loops on hook—a cluster made; (ch 6, make a 5-d tr cluster in next sp, ch 6, cluster over next d tr-group) twice; d tr in next d tr, ch 4, tr in next tr, ch 5, tr in next loop, ch 5, tr in next tr, ch 6, tr in next loop, ch 6, tr in center dc of next 5-dc group, ch 6, tr in next loop, ch 6, tr in next tr, ch 4, tr in next loop. Repeat from * around, ending with ch 3, dc in 4th ch of ch-8. **4th rnd:** Ch 8, dc in next tr, * ch 8, skip next cluster, dc in next loop, (ch 8, sc in next loop) twice; ch 8, dc in next loop, ch 8, skip 1 tr, dc in next tr, ch 8, skip 1 loop, (sc in next loop, ch 8) 4 times; skip 1 loop, dc in next tr. Repeat from * around, ending with ch 4, tr in dc. **5th rnd:** Ch 10, sc in next loop, * ch 10, dc in next loop,. (ch 10, sc in next loop) 3 times; ch 10, dc in next loop, (ch 10, sc in next loop) 5 times. Repeat from * around, ending with ch 5, d tr in tr. **6th and 7th rnds:** * Ch 10, sc in next loop. Repeat from * around, ending with ch 5, d tr in d tr. **8th rnd:** * Ch 12, sc in next loop. Repeat from * around. ending with ch 6, tr tr in last d tr. **9th rnd:** Ch 4, 3-d tr cluster in loop just completed, * ch 12, 4-d tr cluster in next loop. Repeat from * around. Join. **10th rnd:** Sl st in next 6 ch, sc in loop, * ch 12, sc in next loop. Repeat from * around. Join and break off.

PINEAPPLE CENTERPIECE
Continued from page 42.

ch 2 and 2 dc; * (ch 3, sc in next loop) 10 times; ch 3, shell over shell, ch 1, shell in next sp, ch 1, shell over shell. Repeat from * around. Join. **27th rnd:** Shell over shell, * (ch 3, sc in next loop) 9 times; (ch 3, shell over shell) 3 times. Repeat from * around. Join. **28th rnd:** Shell over shell, * (ch 3, sc in next loop) 8 times; ch 3, shell over shell, (ch 4, shell over next shell) twice. Repeat from * around. Join.

29th rnd: Shell over shell, * (ch 3, sc in next loop) 7 times; ch 3, shell over shell, ch 5, in next shell make 2 dc, ch 6 and 2 dc; ch 5, shell over shell. Repeat from * around. **30th rnd:** Shell over shell, * (ch 3, sc in next loop) 6 times; ch 3, shell over shell, ch 3, 16 tr in ch-6 loop, ch 3, shell over shell. Repeat from * around (3rd rnd of pineapples started). Continue to work around until only 1 loop remains at top of 2nd rnd of pineapples. **Next rnd:** Shell over shell, * ch 4, sc in next loop, ch 4, shell over shell, ch 4, sc in next loop, (ch 3, sc in next loop) 11 times; ch 4, shell over shell. Repeat from * around. Join. Now work as follows: **1st rnd:** * Shell over shell, 2 knot sts, shell over shell, ch 4, sc in next ch-3 loop, (ch 3, sc in next loop) 10 times; ch 4. Repeat from * around. Join. **2nd rnd:** * Shell over shell, 2 knot sts, sc under double loop of next knot st (to right of knot), sc under double loop of next knot st (to left of same knot), 2 knot sts, shell over shell, ch 4, sc in next ch-3 loop, (ch 3, sc in next loop) 9 times; ch 4. Repeat from * around. Join. **3rd rnd:** * Shell over shell, (2 knot sts, sc in next 2 double loops—on each side of next knot) twice; 2 knot sts, shell over shell, ch 4, sc in next ch-3 loop, (ch 3, sc in next loop) 8 times; ch 4. Repeat from * around. Join. Continue in this manner, having 1 ch-3 loop less on each row on each pineapple and 2 more knot sts on each knot st section until 1 ch-3 loop remains on each pineapple (there should be 20 knot sts on each knot st section).

Next rnd: Shell over shell, * ch 5, in next knot make (sc, ch 5) 3 times and sc. Repeat from * across knot st section, ch 5, shell over shell, ch 4, sc in next ch-3 loop, ch 4, 2 dc in next shell, ch 1, sl st in sp of last shell, ch 1, 2 dc where last 2 dc were made, ch 5, in next knot make (sc, ch 5) 3 times and sc. Continue thus around, ending with 2 dc in last shell, ch 1, sl st in sp of 1st shell, 2 dc where last 2 dc were made, ch 4, sc in ch-3 loop, ch 4, sl st in top of starting chain. Break off.

Stitches & Abbreviations used in Crocheting

To Increase in Crochet (inc)—Make 2 stitches in one. Always increase in 2nd stitch from edges.

To Decrease in Crochet (dec)—Before working off last loops, insert hook in next stitch and work off loops of both stitches together.

Chain Stitch (ch)—Start with a slip knot on hook. * Thread over and draw through loop on hook. Repeat from * until ch is desired length.

Slip Stitch (sl st)—Insert hook in work, catch thread and draw through work and loop on hook at same time.

Single Crochet (sc)—With a loop on hook, insert hook in work, catch thread and pull through work, thread over again and draw through the 2 loops on hook.

Short Double Crochet (sdc)—Ch for desired length, thread over hook, insert hook in 3rd st from hook, draw thread through (3 loops on hook), thread over and draw through all 3 loops on hook. For succeeding rows, ch 2, turn.

Double Crochet (dc)—Thread over, insert hook in work, catch thread and pull through work, making 3 loops on hook. *Thread over and draw through 2 loops, thread over and draw through remaining 2 loops.

Half Double Crochet (hdc)—Make like dc as far as *, then thread over and draw through all 3 loops on hook at once.

Treble (tr)—Thread over twice, insert hook in work, catch thread and pull through work making 4 loops on hook. Work off in groups of two as in dc. For a **Double Treble (dtr)**, thread over 3 times; for a **Triple Treble (tr tr)**, thread over 4 times; and for a **Long Treble (long tr)**, thread over 5 times; taking off 2 loops at a time as in tr.

Picot (p)—A picot is made on a chain by working a sc in the specified st from hook, taking up 2 loops of ch st,—the left-hand loop and the 1 back loop. A picot is made following a sc, dc, tr, etc., by making the specified number of ch sts, then a sl st in side-top of st preceding chain.

Picot-Loop (p-loop)—This consists of a chain loop with 1 or more picots on it.

Cluster—This consists of 2 or more dc, tr, dtr, or tr tr, gathered together at top into a tight group. Hold the last loop of each st on hook, then thread over and draw through all loops on hook at once, pulling tight.

Open or Filet Mesh (om)—When worked on a chain work the first dc in 8th ch from hook * ch 2, skip 2 sts, in next st, repeat from*. Succeeding rows ch 5 to turn, dc in dc, ch 2, dc in next dc, repeat from *. Sometimes termed **Space (sp).**

Block or Solid Mesh (sm)—Four double crochets form 1 solid mesh and 3 dc are required for each additional solid mesh. Open mesh and solid mesh are used in Filet Crochet. Sometimes termed **Block (bl).**

Bean or Pop Corn Stitch (pc st)—Work 3 dc in same space, drop loop from hook, insert hook in first dc made and draw loop through, ch 1 to tighten st.

Slanting Shell Stitch—Ch for desired length, work 2 dc in 4th st from hook, skip 3 sts, sl st in next st, * ch 3, 2 dc in same st with sl st, skip 3 sts, sl st in next st. Repeat from*. **2nd Row.** Ch 3, turn 2 dc in sl st, sl st in 3 ch loop of shell in previous row, * ch 3, 2 dc in same space, sl st in next shell, repeat from *.

Cross Treble Crochet—Ch for desired length, thread over twice, insert in 5th st from hook, *work off two loops, thread over, skip 2 sts, insert in next st and work off all loops on needle 2 at a time, ch 2, dc in center to complete cross. Thread over twice, insert in next st and repeat from *.

Lacet Stitch—Ch for desired length, work 1 sc in 10th st from hook, ch 3 skip 2 sts, 1 dc in next st, *ch 3, skip 2 sts, 1 sc in next st, ch 3, skip 2 sts 1 dc in next st, repeat from * to end of row. **2nd Row.** Dc in dc, ch 5 dc in next dc.

Knot Stitch—Ch for desired length, * draw a 1/4" loop on hook, thread over and pull through ch, sc in single loop of st draw another 1/4" loop, sc into loop, skip 4 sts, sc in next st, repeat from *. To turn make 3/8" knots, * sc in loop at right of sc and sc in loop at left of sc of previous row, 2 knot sts and repeat from * Sometimes termed **Lover's Knot Stitch.**

OTHER ABBREVIATIONS

sk = Skip
rnd = Round
beg rnd = Beginning round
incl = Inclusive
st = Stitch
sts = Stitches

HELPFUL HINTS

Stitches can be made through either both loops of stitches of previous row or through the back loops only. If not specified, take up both loops.

The term "fasten off" is used whenever the thread is to be cut 6 or 7 inches from the work, slipped through the loop on hook, pulled tight, threaded to a sewing needle and fastened securely on wrong side of work.

* (asterisk) . . . Repeat the instructions following the asterisk as many more times as specified, in addition to the orginal.

Repeat instructions in parentheses as many times as specified. For example: "(ch 5, sc in next sc) 5 times" means to make all that is in parentheses 5 times in all.